Frommer's®

Philadelphia
day BY day

2nd Edition

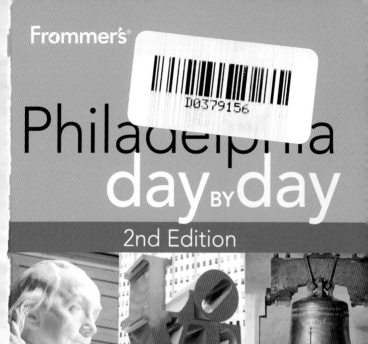

by Reid Bramblett

FrommerMedia LLC

Contents

Published by:

Frommer Media LLC

Copyright © 2014 Frommer Media LLC, New York, NY. All rights reserved. No part of this publication may be reproduced, stored in a retrieval system or transmitted in any form or by any means, electronic, mechanical, photocopying, recording, scanning or otherwise, except as permitted under Sections 107 or 108 of the 1976 United States Copyright Act, without the prior written permission of the Publisher. Requests to the Publisher for permission should be addressed to http://www.frommers.com/support.

Frommer's is a trademark or registered trademark of Arthur Frommer.

ISBN: 978-1-628-87029-9 (paper); 978-1-62887-059-6 (ebk)

Editorial Director: Pauline Frommer
Editor: Anuja Madar
Production Editor: Lindsay Conner
Photo Editor: Seth Olenick
Cartographer: Liz Puhl
Page Compositor: Julie Trippetti
Indexer: Kelly Henthorne
For information on our other products and services, please go to Frommers.com/contactus.

Frommer's also publishes its books in a variety of electronic formats. Some content that appears in print may not be available in electronic formats.

Manufactured in China

5   4   3   2   1

About this Guide

Organizing your time. That's what this guide is all about.

Other guides give you long lists of things to see and do and then expect you to fit the pieces together. The Day by Day guides are different. These guides tell you the best of everything, and then they show you how to see it in the smartest, most time-efficient way. Our authors have designed detailed itineraries organized by time, neighborhood, or special interest. And each tour comes with a bulleted map that takes you from stop to stop.

Hoping to immerse yourself in American history or delve into the amazing art treasures of the Barnes collection? Planning to eat your way through Philly's top culinary hotspots, or tour the iconic Rocky Balboa sites? Whatever your interest or schedule, the Day by Days give you the smartest routes to follow. Not only do we take you to the top attractions, hotels, and restaurants, but we also help you access those special moments that locals get to experience—those "finds" that turn tourists into travelers.

The Day by Days are also your top choice if you're looking for one complete guide for all your travel needs. The best hotels and restaurants for every budget, the greatest shopping values, the wildest nightlife—it's all here.

Why should you trust our judgment? Because our authors personally visit each place they write about. They're an independent lot who say what they think and would never include places they wouldn't recommend to their best friends. They're also open to suggestions from readers. If you'd like to contact them, please send your comments our way at Support@FrommerMedia.com, and we'll pass them on.

Enjoy your Day by Day guide—the most helpful travel companion you can buy. And have the trip of a lifetime.

About the Author

Reid Bramblett is thrilled that, after authoring or contributing to dozens of Frommer's guidebooks over 19 years, he is finally getting to write one about his hometown. He grew up in Cheltenham, on the border of Philadelphia (though he did live at 2nd and Vine in Old City as a child). He has written about travel for everyone from Newsweek, the Miami Herald, and Modern Bride to MSNBC.com, AOL.com, and Travelandleisure.com; served as Associate Editor at Budget Travel magazine; and started his own award-winning Reids-Guides.com family of travel sites. After long stints in New York City, Missouri, and Europe, he has returned to the Philly exurbs of Montgomery County to raise his kids.

An Additional Note

Please be advised that travel information is subject to change at any time—and this is especially true of prices. We therefore suggest that you write or call ahead for confirmation when making your travel plans. The authors, editors, and publisher cannot be held responsible for the experiences of readers while traveling. Your safety is important to us, however, so we encourage you to stay alert and be aware of your surroundings.

Star Ratings, Icons & Abbreviations

Every hotel, restaurant, and attraction listing in this guide has been ranked for quality, value, service, amenities, and special features using a star-rating system. Hotels, restaurants, attractions, shopping, and nightlife are rated on a scale of zero stars (recommended) to three stars (exceptional). In addition to the star-rating system, we also use a **kids** icon to point out the best bets for families. Within each tour, we recommend cafes, bars, or restaurants where you can take a break. Each of these stops appears in a shaded box marked with a coffee-cup-shaped bullet ☕.

The following abbreviations are used for credit cards:

| AE | American Express | DISC | Discover | V | Visa |
| DC | Diners Club | MC | MasterCard | | |

Frommers.com

Frommer's travel resources don't end with this guide. Frommer's website, www.frommers.com, has travel information on more than 4,000 destinations. We update features regularly, giving you access to the most current trip-planning information and the best airfare, lodging, and car-rental bargains. You can also listen to podcasts, connect with other Frommers.com members through our active-reader forums, share your travel photos, read blogs from guide-book editors and fellow travelers, and much more.

A Note on Prices

In the "Take a Break" and "Best Bets" sections of this book, we have used a system of dollar signs to show a range of costs for 1 night in a hotel (the price of a double-occupancy room) or the cost of an entree at a restaurant. Use the following table to decipher the dollar signs:

Cost	Hotels	Restaurants
$	under $130	under $15
$$	$130–$200	$105–$30
$$$	$200–$300	$30–$40
$$$$	$300–$395	$40–$50
$$$$$	over $395	over $50

How to Contact Us

In researching this book, we discovered many wonderful places—hotels, restaurants, shops, and more. We're sure you'll find others. Please tell us about them, so we can share the information with your fellow travelers in upcoming editions. If you were disappointed with a recommendation, we'd love to know that, too. Please write to: Support@FrommerMedia.com

16 Favorite
Moments

16 Favorite Moments

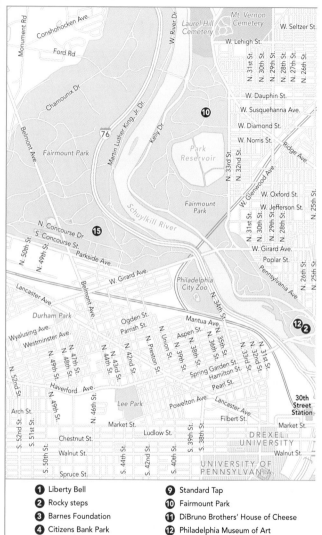

1 Liberty Bell
2 Rocky steps
3 Barnes Foundation
4 Citizens Bank Park
5 Reading Terminal Market
6 Old City
7 La Colombe
8 Independence Park
9 Standard Tap
10 Fairmount Park
11 DiBruno Brothers' House of Cheese
12 Philadelphia Museum of Art
13 Rittenhouse Square
14 City Hall/Broad Street
15 Please Touch Museum
16 Pat's King of Steaks

Previous Page: Children play in a fountain at Logan Circle.

Getting a true feeling for all that is Philadelphia means being willing to embrace extremes. One minute you're immersed in American history, the next you're elbow-to-elbow in a crowd of modern-day foodies. You'll be able to embrace nature at the country's largest city park, glimpse the city's unique brand of chic at Rittenhouse Square, see cutting-edge art in Old City—and, of course, have your fill of that one particular sandwich which many Philadelphians think is as important as Benjamin Franklin (well, almost).

❶ Visit the Liberty Bell. The cracked bell that no longer tolls seems to top every tourist's to-do list. Go see it early, but also walk by it again after dusk, when its bronze cast seems to glow inside its modern glass-and-steel house. *See p 9.*

❷ Run like Rocky up the steps of the Philadelphia Museum of Art. When you get to the top, turn around, pump your fists in the air, and belt out a few bars of "Gonna Fly Now" (or just play it in your head). Then, get your photo taken with the boxer's statue at the foot of the steps. *See p 44.*

❸ Soak in Albert Barnes' amazingly eclectic collection. You'll find an amazing array of work from Matisse (1869–1954), Renoir (1841–1919), Picasso (1881–1973), and Cézanne (1839–1906), plus African sculpture, Pennsylvania Dutch furniture, architectural oddments, and

more in this museum's hip new home on the Parkway. *See p 33.*

❹ Take in a Phillies game. Don't tell, but the Phillies are my favorite of all of the local pro teams, and not just because they brought home the Series in 2008 and went all the way in 2009. Led by soft-spoken sage Charlie Manuel, the Phils have a special vibe that's spirited and modest. Go catch a game at Citizens Bank Park, and when that ball soars "outta here," watch—and hear—the ballpark's giant Liberty Bell ring. *See p 165.*

❺ Get a taste—literally—of Reading Terminal Market. You'll find dozens of local vendors here, boasting every sort of fare Philadelphia has to offer, from oysters and cheesesteaks to cannoli and shoofly pie. Even though it's crazy-packed on Saturday mornings, that's when I like to go, to soak in the hustle and

The Barnes has an unparalleled collection of work by Impressionist painters and others.

The Philadelphia Phillies always attract an energetic crowd to Citizens Bank Park.

bustle—and see what everyone else is buying. *See p 83.*

⑥ Gallery hop Fridays in Old City. Go on the first Friday of the month, and you'll be treated to edgy art, welcoming crowds, and free wine and beer—if you can snag it—mostly along North 2nd and 3rd streets. *See p 50.*

⑦ Order a "cappuccino for here" at La Colombe. For less than $3, you can enjoy a silky foamed coffee in a handsome Deruta cup and discover why *Food and Wine* rated this spot the best cafe in the country. *See p 63.*

⑧ Meet the Colonials. Go ahead. Strike up a chat with the 18th-century characters roaming Independence Park and Old City. Each tricorn-hatted soldier, full-skirted seamstress, fresh-faced page, and dead-ringer for Ben Franklin has an engaging personal story to tell about the birth of the nation. (Plus, they give the best directions.) *See p 26.*

⑨ Drink a pint of hand-pumped ale at Northern Liberties' Standard Tap. You'll be participating in an age-old tradition. Before Prohibition, Philadelphia was the beer-brewing capital of the Western Hemisphere. Today, local microbreweries such as the Philadelphia Brewing Company, Yards, and

Victory are reviving that legacy via delicious stouts, lagers, ambers, pilsners, and more. *See p 122.*

⑩ Walk or bike in Fairmount Park. It's the country's largest city park; my favorite part of it to roam is called Valley Green, with wide pathways, historic bridges, and WPA-era buildings. The area is especially pretty in fall when the leaves change colors and in winter when you can just imagine the horse-and-carriages of yesteryear jingle-belling through the snow. *See p 66.*

La Colombe has been rated the best cafe in the country.

DiBruno Brothers' House of Cheese boasts outstanding cheeses from around the world.

⑪ Cram yourself into the DiBruno Brothers' House of Cheese. The impossibly narrow space in the Italian Market is full of charming cheesemongers who talk you into blowing all your money on an herb-coated raw sheep's milk concoction from the wilds of Provence, or an extra-sharp Provolone aged for two years in Italy. *See p 83.*

⑫ Tour the Museum of Art. For every 50 folks who jog up the Rocky Steps, maybe one bothers going inside the museum itself. Don't lose out on 200 rooms of exquisite works from Old Masters to Impressionists, recreated medieval cloisters to contemporary installations. Come see why this is one of the premier art galleries in North America. *See p 13.*

⑬ Go high-brow along Rittenhouse Square. The time to go is late afternoon to late evening, when a seat at a sidewalk table at one of the seen-and-be-seen watering holes will ensure you a view of the most stylish impromptu parade in town. *See p 47.*

⑭ Catch the Mummers. What Mardi Gras is to New Orleans, this oddly engaging, entirely debauched New Year's Day parade is to Philadelphia, only much chillier and much less organized, if you can picture that. (Imagine a bunch of contractors dressed in sequins, feathers, and face paint, stopping along Broad Street to dance and march to loud pop tunes, and you've got an idea of Mummery.) *See p 20.*

⑮ Let the kids go nuts at Memorial Hall. It may look like an imposing venue, but ever since the Please Touch Museum moved in, it's as welcoming as a playground. Besides reversing the "no touching" rule, it has hundreds of exhibits encouraging kids to play and explore, ride and create, and play some more. *See p 37.*

⑯ Eat a cheesesteak. Preferably at a red picnic table beneath the neon lights at Pat's King of Steaks in South Philly. At 2:30am, just after the bars have all let out. (You didn't think I'd leave this off the list, did you?) *See p 109.* ●

The Best in One Day

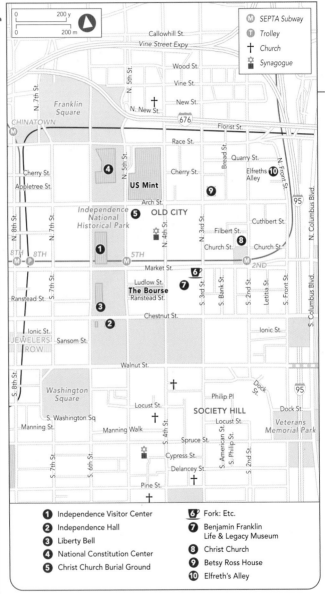

M	SEPTA Subway
T	Trolley
†	Church
☼	Synagogue

0   200 y
0   200 m

Callowhill St.
Vine Street Expy
Wood St.
Vine St.
New St.
N. New St.
CHINATOWN
Franklin Square
Florist St.
Race St.
Cherry St.
Appletree St.
Cherry St.
Quarry St.
Elfreths Alley ⑩
US Mint
Arch St.
Independence National Historical Park ⑤
OLD CITY
Filbert St.
Cuthbert St.
Church St.
Church St.
①
8TH
5TH
Market St.
2ND
Ludlow St.
The Bourse
Ranstead St.
⑥
⑦
③
②
Chestnut St.
Ranstead St.
JEWELERS ROW
Sansom St.
Ionic St.
Walnut St.
Washington Square
Philip Pl
SOCIETY HILL
Dock St.
Locust St.
Locust St.
Veterans Memorial Park
S. Washington Sq
Manning St.
Manning Walk
Spruce St.
Cypress St.
Delancey St.
Pine St.

①	Independence Visitor Center	⑥	Fork: Etc.
②	Independence Hall	⑦	Benjamin Franklin Life & Legacy Museum
③	Liberty Bell	⑧	Christ Church
④	National Constitution Center	⑨	Betsy Ross House
⑤	Christ Church Burial Ground	⑩	Elfreth's Alley

Previous Page: A rendering of The Thinker from the Rodin Museum.

With only a day, focus on the founding of the United States. Philadelphia preserves an astounding number of the buildings, monuments, and even entire streets dating back to the Revolution and beyond. Today the country's "most historic square mile" will be your stomping grounds: Wear comfortable shoes, leave pocket knives at home (security checks), and don't be afraid to chat up the costumed "Colonials." START: **Independence Visitor Center, 6th & Market sts.**

❶ ★★ Independence Visitor Center. This welcome center, with its self-service kiosks, concierge services, umpteen maps and brochures, and box office for tickets to Independence Hall and historic homes isn't just a great first stop for a tour of historic Philadelphia, it's a great first stop for *any* tour of Philadelphia. ◷ ½ hr. 6th & Market sts. ☎ 800/537-7676. www.phlvisitor center.com. Daily from 8:30am.

❷ ★★★ Independence Hall. Where it all went down: the Declaration of Independence, the Articles of Confederation, and the U.S. Constitution. Squeeze into the stately spaces where George Washington (1732–1799), Thomas Jefferson (1743–1826), John Adams (1735–1826), Benjamin Franklin (1706–1790), and their Colonial brethren conceived of a country

affording its citizens "life, liberty and the pursuit of happiness." Don't miss Washington's "Rising Sun Chair," rare maps of the 13 colonies, and the tipstaff (a wooden and brass instrument used to subdue rowdy onlookers in the courtroom). Half-hour tours are guided. ◷ 1 hr.; includes wait in line. Chestnut St., btw. 5th & 6th sts. ☎ 215/965-2305. www.nps.gov/inde. Mar 1–Dec 31, tickets are required (free at Visitor Center or $1.50 in advance online: pick up at least 1 hour before tour). Daily 9am–5pm.

❸ ★★★ Liberty Bell. The cracked, 1-ton symbol of American independence and equality resides in a $12.6-million glass gazebo across Chestnut Street from Independence Hall, preceded by a hall exhaustively documenting it and its role in the Revolution. ◷ ½ hr. Free

Guided tours of Independence Hall leave every half-hour.

The National Constitution Center has performances and interactive exhibits dedicated to the U.S. Constitution.

admission (tickets not required; mandatory security check). Daily 9am–5pm.

❹ ★★ kids National Constitution Center. The newest addition to Independence Park is the world's only museum devoted to the U.S. Constitution—which is way more fun than it sounds. There are live performances in the round that explain the document's history, as well as interactive exhibits that let you take the Presidential Oath of Office, don a Supreme Court robe, stand next to a Declaration signer, and examine hanging chads from the 2000 election. ① 1½ hr. 525 Arch St. ☎ 215/409-6600. www. constitutioncenter.org. Admission $14.50 adults; $13 seniors, students, under 18s; $8 children 4–12. Buy tickets in advance; arrive 20 minutes early for timed theater show. Mon–Fri 9:30am–5pm, Sat 9:30am–6pm, Sun noon–5pm.

❺ ★ Christ Church Burial Ground. The 1719 expansion of Christ Church (bullet ❽) included

the graves of five signers of the Declaration of Independence, one of them Benjamin Franklin. Join the throngs who have tossed a penny on his grave for good luck. ① ¼ hr. SE corner of 5th & Arch sts. www. christchurchphila.org. Mon–Sat 10am–4pm, Sun noon–4pm.

❻ ★★ Fork: Etc. Step back, momentarily, into modern times for a tasty salad, light sandwich, natural soda, cappuccino, and the day's papers at this quick-stop gourmet cafe. For a longer lunch, try Etc.'s slightly more formal sister restaurant, Fork, next door (see p 105). 308 Market St. ☎ 215/625-9425. www.forkrestaurant.com. $–$$.

❼ ★★ kids Benjamin Franklin Life & Legacy Museum. Brick arches disguise Ben Franklin's former home; long ago demolished, its outline is now traced by a steel-girder frame. Surrounding this and

The museum at Franklin Court pays tribute to the man's many careers.

Elfreth's Alley is the oldest continually inhabited street in the United States.

underground is a museum, completely overhauled and reopened in 2013, that pays tribute to the many careers—printer, postmaster, publisher, fireman, scientist, politician—of America's favorite Renaissance Man. Highlights include a replica of Franklin's printing press and a post office that hand-stamps postcards. ① *1 hr. 314–322 Market St.* ☎ *215/965-2305. www.nps.gov/inde. Free admission. Daily 11am–5pm. Post office closed Sun.*

❽ ★★ **Christ Church.** Old City might be proudest of this English Palladian landmark, oft regarded as the neighborhood's most important Colonial building. George Washington had his own pew here. William Penn (1644–1718) received his baptism in the font, a gift from London's All Hallows' Church. In the tiny churchyard is the tomb of Andrew Hamilton, the Philadelphia Lawyer, who helped establish freedom of the press. ① *½ hr. 2nd & Market sts.* ☎ *215/922-1695. www. christchurchphila.org. Free admission. Mon–Sat 9am–5pm; Sun 1–5pm. Closed Mon–Tues in Jan–Feb.*

❾ ★ kids **Betsy Ross House.** The jury's out on whether Betsy Ross (1752–1836), the seamstress of

the Stars and Stripes, actually lived in this teensy abode (or, for that matter, if she really sewed the first flag). No matter: This restored dwelling remains a minute joy to explore, from cellar kitchen to wee bedrooms to flag-filled gift shop. ① *½ hr. 239 Arch St.* ☎ *215/629-4026. www.betsyrosshouse.org. Admission $5 adults, $4 students; audio tour $7. Mar–Nov daily 10am–5pm; Dec–Feb Tues–Sun 10am–5pm.*

❿ ★★★ **Elfreth's Alley.** The oldest continuously inhabited street in the States could teach you a thing or two about getting along with the neighbors. Small, two-story row houses line the narrow cobblestone lane, the original homes of tradesmen, artisans, and urbanites of varied religions and ethnicities. Number 126, the Mantua Maker's House (cape maker), is the alley's museum, complete with 18th-century garden and dressmaker's shop. ① *1 hr. Off 2nd St., toward Front St., btw. Arch & Race sts.* ☎ *215/574-0560. www.elfrethsalley.org. Free admission to visitor center & gift shop; Museum: $5 adults, $1 children (includes 20-minute tour). Tours at noon and 3pm; museum open Wed–Sat 10am–5pm, Sun noon–5pm.*

The Best **in Two Days**

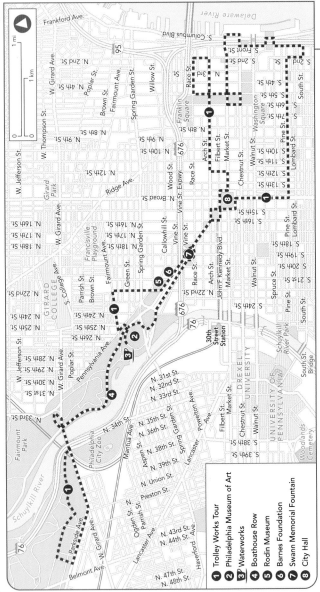

1 Trolley Works Tour
2 Philadelphia Museum of Art
3 Waterworks
4 Boathouse Row
5 Rodin Museum
6 Barnes Foundation
7 Swann Memorial Fountain
8 City Hall

Y**ou've done enough walking.** On day two, it's time to take a load off and get the lay of the land (and visit some top sights) with a ride around Old City, Center City, Museum Mile, Penn's Landing, and Fairmount Park aboard a Victorian-style trolley. START: **5th & Market sts, or any of the 21 stops along the trolley's route.**

❶ ★★ kids **Trolley Works Tour.** A 24-hour pass for the surprisingly speedy rail-less trolleys and double-decker buses gets you the most comprehensive tour of downtown. On-and-off privileges and unlimited rides mean if Junior wants to see **Eastern State Penitentiary** (see p 48, bullet ❽) again, or if you regret not grabbing those vintage earrings on Antique Row, a second chance is just a short ride away. (The route is also plied by their double decker buses.) 🕐 *1½ hr. 5th & Market sts.; 20 more stops along route, plus shuttles from hotels.* ☎ *215/389-8687. www. phillytour.com. 24-hour pass: $27 adults, $25 seniors, $10 children. Apr–Nov daily 9:30am–5pm (to 6pm weekends July–Aug); Dec–Mar daily 10am–4pm.*

❷ ★★★ **Philadelphia Museum of Art.** Hop off at this Greco-Roman temple on a hill, jog up the steps à la Rocky, and get lost in 200 galleries of art and objets, medieval cloisters, and blockbuster special exhibitions. Among the more than quarter-million works are Cézanne's (1839–1906) monumental *Bathers*, paintings by native Philadelphian Thomas Eakins (1844–1916), and classics from Van Gogh (1853–1890), Poussin (1594–1665), Rubens (1577–1640), Duchamp (1887–1968), and Monet (1840–1926). Head across the street to the new Perelman Building for cutting-edge works by Marcel Wanders (b. 1963) and Frank Gehry (b. 1929). 🕐 *2 hrs. 26th St. & Ben Franklin Pkwy.* ☎ *215/763-1000. www.philamuseum.org. Admission $20 adults, $18 seniors, $14 students (does not include special exhibits); first Sun of the month (and Wed after 5pm), pay what you wish. Admission also covers Perelman Building and Rodin Museum. Tues–Sun 10am–5pm (Wed & Fri until 8:45pm).*

The Philadelphia Museum of Art features more than 200 galleries.

Philadelphia Museum of Art

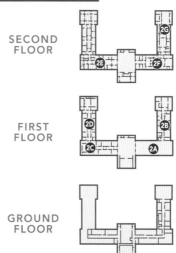

SECOND FLOOR

FIRST FLOOR

GROUND FLOOR

You'll spend most of your time on the first and second floors of this U-shaped museum. Begin where your interests lie—especially at **Ⓐ Special Exhibitions,** which are almost always world-class, usually require advance reservations, and charge additional admission. Next, explore works by Thomas Eakins, as well as Shaker and Pennsylvania Dutch furnishings in the **Ⓑ American Collection.** Cross the grand stairs (looking up to see Alexander Calder's [1898–1976] *Ghost* mobile) to **Ⓒ European Art** 1850–1900, packed with works representative of the Impressionist, Symbolist, Naturalist, and Art Nouveau styles including works by Cézanne, Cassatt

(1844–1926), Monet, Van Gogh, and amazing period objets. Before you head upstairs, take a quick spin through **Ⓓ Modern and Contemporary Art** for iconoclastic pieces by Jasper Johns (b. 1930), Cy Twombly (b. 1928), Constantin Brancusi (1876–1957), and Marcel Duchamp. The second floor shows earlier pieces from Europe: **Ⓔ 1500–1850 French and English period rooms,** with works by Poussin and Rubense; **Ⓕ 1100–1500: Renaissance works** including a 15th-century Venetian bedroom, a French Gothic chapel; and an **Ⓖ Asian gallery** that includes an interesting mix: a Japanese teahouse, Persian carpets, and a 16th-century Indian temple hall.

3 ★ Waterworks. Just behind the museum, a 200-year-old municipal water system has been cleverly restored as an elegant river-top restaurant. Try the Maine lobster BLT and a bottle from the water list. *640 Water Works Dr.* ☎ *215/236-9000.* www.thewaterworksrestaurant.com. Closed Mon. $–$$$.

❹ ★★ **Boathouse Row.** From the restaurant, head toward the river, along Kelly Drive, to this iconic row of 10 antique (circa 1850s–1870s) clubhouses belonging to collegiate and other amateur crew groups and teams. You'll likely glimpse some oarsmen sculling along the river. Come back, if you can, after dark to see the houses lit up. ⏱ ½ hr.

❺ ★★★ **Rodin Museum.** Farther up the Parkway, stop by this Paul Cret–designed mini-museum where *The Thinker* and the *Gates of Hell* greet you to the largest collection of Rodin's (1840–1917) works outside of Paris. It's a lovely spot, replete with major sculptures, plaster models, and original sketchbooks. ⏱ 1 hr. 2151 Ben Franklin Pkwy (at 22nd St). ☎ 215/763-8100. www.rodinmuseum.org. Suggested admission $8 adults, $7 seniors, $6 students (or free with Art Museum ticket; above). Wed–Mon 10am–5pm.

❻ ★★★ **Barnes Foundation.** Moved here (contentiously) from its original suburban home in 2012, this world-renowned museum is stuffed with some 8,000 largely Impressionist and Post-Impressionist works (Renoir, Cézanne, Matisse, Picassos, Van Gogh) fussily arranged by Barnes himself alongside antique everyday objects (think: iron hinges) and primitive sculpture. ⏱ 2 hrs. 2025 Benjamin Franklin Pkwy. ☎ 215/278-7000. www.barnesfoundation.org. Reservations highly recommended. Admission $22 adults. Wed–Thurs & Sat–Mon 10am–6pm; Fri 10am–10pm.

❼ ★ **Swann Memorial Fountain.** A few more blocks and you'll run into Logan Circle and its classical centerpiece fountain. Also known as "The Fountain of the Three Rivers," the aquatic sculpture

The clubhouses along Boathouse Row date back to the mid-19th century.

represents the region's three major waterways: the Schuylkill, Delaware, and Wissahickon. It was created by Alexander Stirling Calder (1870–1945), father of Alexander Calder (he of the giant mobile in the Art Museum) and son of City Hall sculptor Alexander Milne Calder. ⏱ 20 min. 1 Logan Sq., at 18th St. & Ben Franklin Pkwy.

❽ ★★ **City Hall.** Until 1987, the 37-foot, 27-ton bronze statue of Philly founder William Penn—created by Alexander Milne Calder (1846–1923), as was all the statuary on this, the world's largest unsupported masonry building—remained the highest point in Philadelphia at 548 feet. In fact, City Hall briefly reigned as the world's tallest building (1901–08). It remains the largest municipal building in the U.S., with 14½ acres of office space. Worth it: Views from the tower observation deck (Mon–Fri 9:30am–4:15pm). Interesting: the 2-hour tour (Mon–Fri at 12:30pm). City Hall is surrounded by Dilworth Plaza, remade into a public space in 2013 with a concert lawn, cafe, and fountain that doubles as a winter ice rink. ⏱ 20–60 min. Broad & Market sts.

The Best **in Three Days**

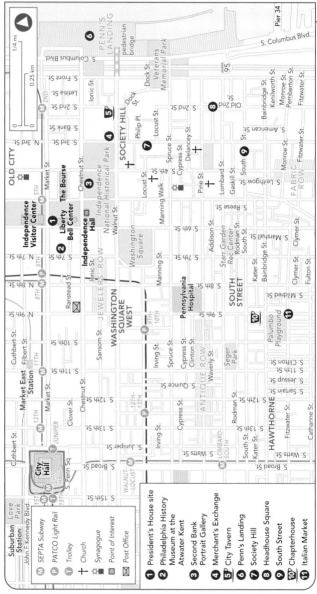

Suburban Station
Love Park
John F. Kennedy Blvd.

Ⓜ SEPTA Subway
Ⓟ PATCO Light Rail
Ⓣ Trolley
✝ Church
✡ Synagogue
■ Point of Interest
⊠ Post Office

❶ President's House site
❷ Philadelphia History Museum at the Atwater Kent
❸ Second Bank Portrait Gallery
❹ Merchant's Exchange
❺ City Tavern
❻ Penn's Landing
❼ Society Hill
❽ Headhouse Square
❾ South Street
🔟 Chapterhouse
⓫ Italian Market

It's time to get to know the city's inimitable blend of gorgeous, gritty, and gourmet that makes Philadelphia . . . Philly.
START: **Southeast corner of 6th St. & Market St.**

❶ ★ President's House site.
This open-air mock-up of low walls and hovering windows and door frames replicates America's first "white house," a three-story brick mansion George Washington called "the best single house in the city," where both he (1790–1797) and John Adams (1797–1800) lived and worked as President. Plaques and videos give insights on everything from Presidential duties to the lives of the slaves who worked here; in a few spots you can peer at excavations of the actual house's remains. ⏱ *20 min. Market St. at S. 6th St. www.nps.gov/inde. Admission free. Always open.*

❷ ★ Philadelphia History Museum at the Atwater Kent.
The only museum to Philly itself details the birth and continuing life of the city via sublime art and amazing objects spanning early Quaker fashions to Norman Rockwell works to 2008 Phillies memorabilia. Don't miss the giant, walk-upon floor map detailing Philly's every natural and man-made nook and cranny. ⏱ *1 hr. 15 S. 7th St. (between Chestnut and Market sts.)* ☎ *215/685-4830. www.philadelphiahistory.org. Admission $10 adults; $8 seniors, $6 students; free 12 and under. Tues–Sat 10:30am–4:30pm.*

❸ ★ Second Bank Portrait Gallery. William Strickland designed this impressive, time-bitten Greek Revival structure to house the influential Second Bank of the United States in 1816. It now houses excellent paintings of famous early Americans (some by noted portraitist Charles Wilson Peale), from Ben Franklin and Patrick Henry to explorers Lewis and

The Second Bank of the U.S. is now a national portrait gallery.

Clark. ⏱ *45 min. 420 Chestnut St. (btw. 4th & 5th sts.)* ☎ *215/965-2305. www.nps.gov/inde. Admission free. Wed–Sat 10am–5pm.*

❹ Merchant's Exchange. The oldest stock exchange building in the U.S. was another Greek Revival Strickland special from the 1830s, now the offices of Independence Hall National Park. Check out the back's curved colonnade. ⏱ *5 min. Walnut, 3rd, & Dock sts.*

5 ★ City Tavern. This faithful reconstruction of the original pub where the Fathers of our Country hashed out the details of the Declaration and Constitution over tankards of ale still serves many 18th century dishes, from West Indies pepperpot soup to salmagundi to

Colonial turkey pot pie. *620 138 S. 2nd St. (at Walnut St.).* ☎ *215/413-1443. www.citytavern.com. $$.*

⑥ Penn's Landing. No longer a bustling port, the pedestrian-friendly Delaware Riverfront is now a relaxing place to stroll. If you're into seafaring, visit the **Independence Seaport Museum** (see p 57, bullet ⑫) and some of the historic ships anchored here: the 1892 *USS Olympia* (oldest steel warship afloat); the 1944 *USS Becuna* (the only Guppy 1-A sub on display; she served in World War II, Korea, and Vietnam—when not shadowing Soviet subs); and the four-masted tall ship *Moshulu,* now a restaurant (see p 96). Afterward, walk south past the Art Deco–inspired Hyatt Regency, then cross back over Columbus Boulevard at Spruce Street. ⏲ *90min. Columbus Blvd at Walnut St. www.delawareriverwaterfrontcorp.com.*

⑦ ★★ Society Hill. Back on the "mainland," shudder briefly at I.M. Pei's hideous Society Hill Towers (1963), then turn south into the quiet streets lined by brick Colonial-, Georgian-, and Federal-style townhouses—one of the city's first residential neighborhoods, and still among its finest. (For a neighborhood walk and more details, see p 54.) ⏲ *½ hr. 244 S. 3rd St.*

⑧ Headhouse Square. This all-brick replica of the original "New Market" or "Shambles" is once again (Sun May–Dec) an open-air farmers market under continuous, English-style sheds. At its north end is the nation's oldest surviving volunteer firehouse. ⏲ *15 min. 2nd St., btw. Pine & Lombard sts.*

South Street is a beacon to the city's youth.

⑨ South Street. For decades, this colorful strip of sneaker stores, costume jewelers, rustic cafes, and cheap eats has been Mecca for Philly's under-21 set. Make sure you cross 10th Street to see the mosaic wonderland of Isaiah Zagar's Philadelphia's Magic Gardens at no. 1020 (www.philadelphiasmagicgardens.org). ⏲ *15 min.*

⑩ ★★ Chapterhouse. This airy and art-dappled converted storefront serves espressos, smoothies, and pastries to a crowd of med students and neighborhood types. Or save your noshing for the Italian Market. *620 S. 9th St. (btw. South & Bainbridge sts.).* ☎ *215/238-2626. $.*

⑪ ★★ Italian Market. The mix of old-school Italian vendors of meats, cheeses, pastries, and produce—along with Mexican bodegas and taquerías, and junk shops galore—in the "oldest outdoor market in America" is nothing if not vibrant.

Italian/9th Street Market

A **Sarcone's** (758 S. 9th St.) has been turning out crusty sesame-seed loaves, garlicky tomato pies, and pepperoni stuffed breads since 1918. **B Isgro's Pastry** (1009 Christian St.) bakes amazing pine-nut cookies and cannoli. **C Fiorella's** (817 Christian St.) makes sausage, right in front of you. **D D'Angelo Bros.** (909 S. 9th St.) butcher has seriously wild game. **E The Spice Corner** (904 S. 9th St.) offers bargain flavorings. The **F mural of former mayor Frank Rizzo** (just past Salter St. in parking lot on the right) is Philly's most defaced public art. Head to **G Claudio's** (922–924 S. 9th St.) for olives, charcuterie, and house-made mozzarella. **H DiBruno Brothers' House of Cheese** (930 S. 9th St.) is the market's most vaunted kiosk for amazing cheeses. **I Fante's** (1006 S. 9th St.) offers a cookware and bakeware bonanza. **J Giordano's** (1041–1043 S. 9th St.) has cheap produce out front, cheap parmesan and provolone in back. A few blocks south, on opposing corners of S. 9th Street & Passyunk Avenue, is Philly's ultimate (most say overrated) cheesesteak smack-down spot: **K Geno's** is the neon half of the duel; **L Pat's King of Steaks** is the other, claiming original sandwich cred. ⏱ *2–3 hrs.* ☎ *215/278-2903. www.italianmarketphilly.org. 9th St. btw. Fitzwater & Federal sts. Mon–Sat 8am–4pm; Sun 8am–1pm.*

Keeping Mum

If you thought the Italian Market was gritty, you ain't seen nothing 'til you've seen the **Mummers' Museum.** This unintentionally oddball homage to Philly's New Year's Day parade (think Mardi Gras with more feathers, fewer beads, less organization) encapsulates a local tradition that's virtually ineffable, but here goes . . . Every January 1, hundreds of locals who've spent the previous year rehearsing routines, concocting opulently clownish costumes and over-the-top sets, and spray-painting shoes gold, "perform" (dance, play instruments, stumble while intoxicated) up Broad Street. The parade descends, apparently, from an old wassailing-style tradition. But this spot, with its strange decor and old-to-quite-old memorabilia, feels more eccentric than historic—in a good way, of course. ① ½ hr. 1100 2nd St. (at Washington Ave.) ☎ 215/336-3050. www.mummersmuseum.com. Admission $3.50 adults, $2.50 seniors & children. Wed–Sat 9:30am–4:30pm. ●

Penn's Landing is home to the four-masted tall ship Moshulu, *now a restaurant.*

Philadelphia Early America

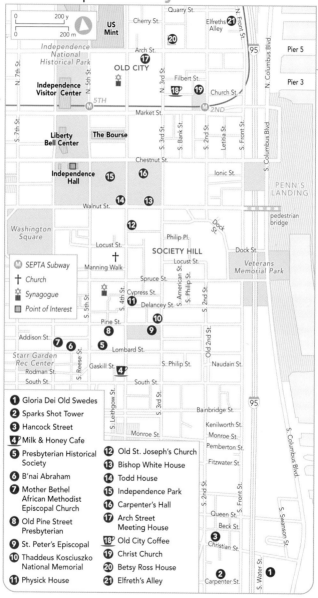

- **1** Gloria Dei Old Swedes
- **2** Sparks Shot Tower
- **3** Hancock Street
- **4** Milk & Honey Cafe
- **5** Presbyterian Historical Society
- **6** B'nai Abraham
- **7** Mother Bethel African Methodist Episcopal Church
- **8** Old Pine Street Presbyterian
- **9** St. Peter's Episcopal
- **10** Thaddeus Kosciuszko National Memorial
- **11** Physick House
- **12** Old St. Joseph's Church
- **13** Bishop White House
- **14** Todd House
- **15** Independence Park
- **16** Carpenter's Hall
- **17** Arch Street Meeting House
- **18** Old City Coffee
- **19** Christ Church
- **20** Betsy Ross House
- **21** Elfreth's Alley

Previous page: Kids enjoy the goat sculpture at Rittenhouse Square.

I t can be easy to forget that the quest for religious freedom inspired the founding of the United States. To early Americans, churches were more than places to worship—they were symbols of liberation. This tour includes some of the city's oldest churches and houses-turned-museums. START: **Gloria Dei Old Swedes, Columbus Blvd. & Christian St.**

Gloria Dei Old Swedes is the oldest church in Pennsylvania (and still active).

1 ★★ Gloria Dei Old Swedes. Established in 1700, this still-active Episcopal parish is the second-oldest church in the U.S., a legacy of the short-lived Delaware Valley colony of New Sweden (which predated the British settlements). This 18th-century microcosm is complete with a mini parish hall, rectory, and graveyard. Two models of ships that carried the first Swedish settlers to these shores in 1638 hang inside the church. In the vestry is a silver crown that any woman married here (as was Betsy Ross) may wear at her wedding. Old maps star in the one-room museum. ⏱ *½ hr. Christian St. at Columbus Blvd.* ☎ *215/389-1513. www.old-swedes.org. Free admission. Daily 9am–4pm (closed Monday Labor Day–Memorial Day).*

2 Sparks Shot Tower. That smokestack-looking thing towering over a neighborhood park is the oldest shot tower in the U.S., opened on July 4, 1808. This 142-foot brick pillar produced shots for the War of 1812 and Civil War via a brilliantly simple process. Molten lead was poured through a copper sieve near the top. The lead dripped out in perfect spheres (thanks to surface tension), which were solidified by the rushing air as each drop fell into a water basin at the bottom. ⏱ *1 min. 129–131 Carpenter St. No admission.*

3 ★ Hancock Street. One of the many dozens of Center City's pretty tree-lined alleys, this street is bordered by tiny houses called "trinities"—one floor each for faith, hope, and charity. While walking around the city, take small cobblestone streets like this to escape traffic and feel a tad bit more Colonial. ⏱ *10 min.*

★ **Milk & Honey Cafe.** Always busy, this eclectic cafe—formerly Philadelphia Java Co., where Charlie begins stalking The Waitress in It's Always Sunny in Philadelphia—has yummy sandwiches and ice cream. *518 S. 4th St. (btw. South & Lombard sts.).* ☎ *215/928-1811. $.*

⑤ Presbyterian Historical Society. The oldest denominational archives in the U.S. (est. 1852) are 30,000 cubic feet of documents tracing the history of American Presbyterians. Worth a pause to admire their sheer existence. ⏱ *2 min. 435 Lombard St.* ☎ *215/627-1852. www.history.pcusa.org. Free admission.*

⑥ B'nai Abraham. The oldest synagogue in Philly was founded in 1874 by Russian Jews fleeing Tsar Alexander II—though the current building dates to 1910. ⏱ *1 min. 527 Lombard St.* ☎ *215/238-2100. www.phillyshul.com.*

⑦ ★ Mother Bethel African Methodist Episcopal Church. On the oldest piece of American soil continuously owned by African-Americans is the mother church of

Old Pine Street Presbyterian is known as "the church of the patriots."

African Methodist Episcopalism, a faith practiced by 2.5 million. Dedicated in 1794 by pastor Richard Allen (1760–1831), who bought his own freedom from slavery, the handsome current church was built in 1890. Mother Bethel houses Allen's tomb, his Bible, and his hand-hewn pulpit—all available for view by appointment only. ⏱ *½ hr. 419 S. 6th St. (btw. Pine & Lombard sts.).* ☎ *215/925-0616. www.mother bethel.org. Free admission.*

⑧ ★ Old Pine Street Presbyterian. The city's oldest standing (circa 1768) Presbyterian church offers a glimpse of Colonial design—the hand-painted stencils are particularly lovely—and an idea of how John Adams (1735–1826) spent his Sundays. In 1774, pastor George Duffield (1732–1790) was chaplain to the First Continental Congress. In 1776 and 1777, he served under George Washington (1732–1799) during the harsh winter at Valley Forge, making Old Pine known as the "church of the patriots." Buried in the churchyard are 50-some Revolutionary War soldiers, a signer of the Constitution, and a ringer of the Liberty Bell. ⏱ *½ hr. 412 Pine St.* ☎ *215/925-8051. www.oldpine.org. Free admission.*

⑨ ★ St. Peter's Episcopal. West of Old Pine rises the William Strickland–designed steeple of this ornate 1761 church once attended by George Washington (he sat in box pew 41). Buried in the churchyard are Col. John Nixon, who first read the Declaration of Independence to the public on July 8, 1776; Charles Wilson Peale (1741–1827), portraitist of George Washington; Vice-President George Mifflin Dallas (1792–1864), for whom Dallas, Texas, was named; and Commodore Stephen Decatur (1779-1820), hero of Tripoli. ⏱ *½ hr. 313 Pine St.*

The Thaddeus Kosciuszko National Memorial pays tribute to a Polish hero of the American Revolution.

☎ 215/925-5968. www.stpeters phila.org. Free admission.

⑩ ★★ Thaddeus Kosciuszko National Memorial. One of the great foreign heroes of the Revolution, Thaddeus Kosciuszko (1746–1817) came to Philadelphia from Poland in 1776—just in time to read the Declaration, befriend Thomas Jefferson (1743–1826), and fortify the city. Before that glory, he occupied a room in this Georgian-style boardinghouse, a dwelling he'd requested to be "as small, as remote, and as cheap" as possible. 🕐 ½ hr. 310 Pine St. ☎ 215/597-9618. www.nps.gov/thko. Free admission. Sat–Sun noon–4pm (hours may expand if federal sequester ends).

⑪ ★ Physick House. Built in 1786 and inhabited by Philip Syng Physick, "The Father of American Surgery" (and inventor of soda). For more, see p 56. 🕐 40 min. 321 S. 4th St. (at Delancey St.). ☎ 215/925-7866. www.philalandmarks.org. Admission $5 adults, $4 seniors & students. Thurs–Sat noon–4pm; Sun 1–4pm (Jan-Feb by appointment only).

⑫ ★ Old St. Joseph's Church. At the time this Jesuit church was founded in 1733, it was the only place in the English-speaking world where Roman Catholics could celebrate Mass publicly. Among its worshippers was General Lafayette (1757–1834). The building's unassuming facade is intentional: Ben Franklin (1706–1790) advised

The elegant Bishop White House is circa 1786.

Founding Father John Greaton (1741–1783) to disguise the church for protection against acts of religious intolerance—though the interior has been restored (after anti-Catholic riots in the 1830s) to its Colonial glory. ○ *20 min. 321 Willings Alley (4th St., near Walnut St.).* ☎ *215/923-1733. www.oldst joseph.org. Free admission.*

⓭ ★★ Bishop White House.

Dr. William White (1783–1815) was a community pillar in Federal America: founder of the breakaway Episcopal Church; rector of St. Peter's and Christ Church; chaplain to the Second Continental Congress; and pal to Franklin, Washington, and Adams. His elegant, circa-1786 house is decidedly upper-class, from its painted cloth floor to its unusually stocked second-floor library and its indoor "necessary"— a novelty in its time. You can get tickets for the required tours (which include the Todd House, below) at the Independence Visitor Center. ○ *½ hr. 309 Walnut St.* ☎ *215/965-2305. www.nps.gov/inde. Free admission. Temporarily closed at press time due to federal sequestration cuts; normal hours: Daily 10am–4pm.*

⓮ ★ Todd House.

John Todd, Jr. was a young Quaker lawyer of moderate means. In his circa-1775 Georgian dwelling, the first floor was his office, and his family lived and entertained on the second floor. Todd died in the 1793 yellow fever epidemic. His widow Dolley married future President James Madison (1751–1836). ○ *½ hr. 4th & Walnut sts.* ☎ *215/965-2305. www.nps.gov/inde. Free admission. Temporarily closed at press time due to federal sequestration cuts; normal hours: Daily 10am–4pm.*

⓯ ★★★ kids Independence Park.

"America's most historic

Todd House was home to a young Quaker lawyer whose widow married President James Madison.

square mile" is home to Independence Hall and the Liberty Bell. (See p 4, bullet ❶.) In summer, actors in 18th-century costumes roam this area, performing as rabble rousers, muster leaders, and storytellers. Some teach kids to march or roll hoops. Check online for scheduling details, or grab a bench and see what happens. ○ *1 hr. www.historicphiladelphia.org.*

⓰ ★ Carpenter's Hall.

In 1774, delegates from 12 of the 13 colonies gathered at this neutral meeting spot, home to the trade guild that erected Independence Hall and Christ Church, for the First Continental Congress. They spent 7 weeks drafting 10 resolutions that declared the rights of the Colonies to the British King and Parliament— the precedent to the Declaration of Independence. Carpenter's Hall remains the club for architects, builders, and structural engineers. ○ *½ hr. 320 Chestnut St.* ☎ *215/925-0167. www.carpenters hall.com. Free admission. Tues–Sun 10am–4pm (closed Tues Jan–Feb).*

⑰ ★ Arch Street Meeting House. This plain brick building dates from 1804, but William Penn (1644–1718) gave the land to his Religious Society of Friends—a.k.a. Quakers—in 1693. Quakers believe in a plain and hierarchy-free style of worship referred to as a "meeting." Weekly meetings include much silent meditation until a "Friend" is moved to speak. ① *10 min. 4th & Arch sts.* ☎ *215/627-2667. www. archstreetfriends.org. Free admission.*

⑱ ★ Old City Coffee. This charming cafe is the perfect spot to revive with a double espresso, iced green tea, or homemade coffee cake. *221 Church St.* ☎ *215/629-9292. www.oldcitycoffee.com. $.*

⑲ ★★ Christ Church. Another church, but the most prominent on the list, this landmark Colonial structure—one of the country's finest examples of Georgian architecture—is a quick visit, where you'll see the pews of many a Declaration signer. (See p 11, bullet ⑧.) ① *½ hr. 2nd & Market sts. Free admission.*

⑳ ★ kids Betsy Ross House. After all, one of these houses ought to be known for its famous female resident. This twee residence may have belonged to Betsy Ross

Independence Park features statues (and actors) in colonial garb.

(1752–1836), the woman who may have designed and sewn the nation's first flag (the jury's still out on both questions). (See p 11, bullet ⑨.) ① *½ hr. 239 Arch St. Free admission.*

㉑ ★★★ Elfreth's Alley. In the shadow of the Ben Franklin Bridge, Elfreth's Alley remains the longest continuously inhabited street in America. Along this sun-dappled cobblestone residential lane is a house converted to a museum and garden. (See p 51, bullet ④.) ① *½ hr. Off 2nd St., toward Front St., btw. Arch & Race sts.*

The resolutions decided on in 1774 at Carpenter's Hall formed the precedent to the Declaration of Independence.

Art Philly-Style

0   200 y
0   200 m

Ⓜ SEPTA Subway
Ⓣ Trolley
† Church

1 Clothespin
2 Your Move
3 Pennsylvania Academy of the Fine Arts
4 Lenfest Plaza (Cherry Street)
5 Love Park
6 Milk & Honey
7 Swann Memorial Fountain
8 Barnes Foundation
9 Rodin Museum
10 Washington Monument
11 Philadelphia Museum of Art
12 Perelman Building

The grand Philadelphia Museum of Art and the rich, eclectic Barnes are the stars of the local art scene. Still, any tour of the city is an art tour, thanks to a 1959 mandate that all new building projects dedicate 1% of construction costs to public art. Consider such serendipitous finds PDAs—public displays of art-fection. START: **City Hall, 15th & Market sts.**

Claes Oldenburg's famous "Clothespin" statue.

❶ ★ *Clothespin.* One of Philadelphia's many public displays of art is Claes Oldenburg's (b. 1929)

10-ton, 45-foot-tall, circa-1976 tribute to, yes, laundry, but also to Brancusi's (1876–1957) *The Kiss.* Across from City Hall (see p 60, bullet ❹), this sculpture is a feat of imagination and engineering— notice how the *Clothespin* isn't quite closed—and not without its critics. ⏱ *10 min. 15th & Market sts.*

❷ ★ kids *Your Move.* It's no coincidence that Daniel Martinez's (b. 1957) colossal game pieces—an iron from Monopoly; dominoes; and "men" from Parcheesi, checkers, and chess—are located directly across from City Hall. The hodgepodge juxtaposes childhood pastimes and adult responsibilities—and offers a nice spot for a photo. ⏱ *10 min. Broad St & JFK Blvd.*

❸ ★★★ **Pennsylvania Academy of the Fine Arts.** Two blocks north of City Hall stands the

Daniel Martinez's "Your Move" is located directly across from City Hall.

Mural Capital of the World

Philadelphia is home to more than 3,600 official murals—and untold numbers of non-sanctioned ones as well. When, in 1984, Mayor Wilson Goode hired artist Jane Golden to help purge the city of the graffiti plague, they employed a radical tactic: **The Mural Arts Program** (☎ 215/925-3633; www.muralarts.org). Rather than hounding graffiti artists and painting over their tags—which would only give them a fresh canvas—Golden enlisted them. Now, instead of breaking the law to practice their art, they were being paid by the city to create; to give their neighborhoods and their struggles a voice; to beautify the city and proudly showcase its diversity. From job skills training to prison programs to an arts education effort serving 1,800 youths annually, Mural Arts has been a wild success. Visit the website for more information and to sign up for highly recommended tours (by trolley, bike, foot, car—or even participatory).

country's first art museum, which also happens to be the country's first fine arts school. Known by its acronym, PAFA occupies a beautifully restored, circa-1876 High Victorian Gothic building designed by architects Frank Furness (1839–1912) and George W. Hewitt (1841–1916). Presidential portraitist Charles Willson Peale (1741–1827) and early American sculptor William Rush (1756–1833) founded the Academy in 1805. American realist Thomas Eakins (1844–1916) studied and taught here. All three artists were Philadelphians, and all are well represented among the gallery's thousands of all-American works. Of special note: Furness' splendid red, gold, and blue staircase; an elegant rotunda where Walt Whitman (1819–1892) attended concerts; Benjamin West's (1738–1820) *Penn's Treaty with the Indians;* Peale's paintings of Franklin and Washington; rare works by Rush; and pieces by more modern American artists such as Mark Rothko (1903–1970), Robert Motherwell (1915–1991), Georgia

O'Keefe (1887–1986), Edward Hopper (1882–1967), Andrew Wyeth (1917–2009), and Robert Rauschenberg (1925–2008). ⏱ *2 hr. 118 N. Broad St.* ☎ *215/972-7600. www. pafa.org. Admission to permanent collection $15 adults, $12 seniors &*

Meg Saligman's "Common Threads" is part of the city's Mural Arts program.

The Pennsylvania Academy of the Fine Arts is the country's first art museum and its first arts school.

students with ID, $8 youth 13–18; 12 and under free. (Free admission to ground-floor gallery). Tues–Sat 10am–5pm, Sun 11am–5pm. Free tours Tues, Thurs–Fri 11:30am & 12:30pm, Wed, Sat–Sun 1pm & 2pm.

④ ★ Lenfest Plaza (Cherry Street). Claes Oldenburg strikes again! In the summer of 2011, the 51-foot Paint Torch was raised as an exclamation point to this suddenly pedestrian-only block of Cherry Street between the two buildings of PAFA. Everyone likes to climb on the dollop of orange paint that "dripped" from the oversized brush to the sidewalk below. Beyond it may still find an artfully crumpled Grumman Tracker II plane turned into a greenhouse by Jordan Griska; meant to be a temporary installation but at press time it was still standing. ⏱ *10 min. Cherry St. (btw. N. Broad and N. 15th sts.)*

⑤ ★★ Love Park. Robert Indiana's (b. 1928) bright red, font-based work is one of the most iconic monuments in the City of Brotherly Love, even though duplicates exist throughout the world. Still, as centerpiece of this lovingly planted park (a former haven for urban skateboarders), it serves as a gentle reminder of all we need. ⏱ *15 min. 15th St. & JFK Blvd.*

⑥ ★ Milk & Honey. In 2012, this West Philly locavore market opened a cafe in Sister Cities Park on the east side of Logan Circle. The panini are made with artisanal cheese and meats, farmers market veggies, and locally baked bread. Also: cookies, cupcakes, and Bassett's ice cream. *200 N 18th St. (at Logan Sq.)* ☎ *215/665-8600. www.milkandhoneymarket.com. $.*

First Fridays: Galleries Galore

Every "First Friday" of the month, the independent art galleries of Old City stay open late to debut exhibits and to serve wine in little plastic cups to enthused, mostly youthful, crowds. If you happen to be in town on a First Friday, get to **Old City** early (gallery usually open 5–9pm for the event; www.oldcityarts.org), start your exploration north of Market Street along 2nd or 3rd, and have at it. Also, if you're planning to dine after you wine, and if you'd like to remain in the neighborhood, be sure to make dinner reservations. On a typical Friday night, Old City is Philly's busiest area. On a First Friday, it's busier still.

❼ ★★ kids Swann Memorial Fountain. Back along Ben Franklin Parkway—occasionally referred to as Philly's Champs-Élysées—are more examples of public artwork, especially sculpture. This grand, classical fountain, with ornate horses and mile-high water,

The Swann Memorial Fountain, created by Alexander Stirling Calder.

represents the city's three major waterways. It is the work of Philadelphian Alexander Stirling Calder (1870–1945), son of Alexander Milne Calder (1846–1923)—who did the hundreds of statues festooning City Hall just down the road, including Billy Penn—and father of Alexander Calder (1898–1976), who made the mobile in the Art Museum. The fountain serves as a summer splashing spot for local kids. ⏲ ½ hr. Logan Sq. (19th & Race sts).

❽ ★★★ Barnes Foundation. Moved (contentiously) from its home in the suburbs in 2012 to anchor this new Museum Mile along the Parkway, this world-renowned museum was the life's work of prescient collector Albert Barnes (1872–1951), a pharmaceutical tycoon who amassed 8,000 works, including 181 Renoirs, 69 Cézannes, 59 Matisses, 46 Picassos (1881–1973), Pennsylvania "Dutch" furniture, primitive sculpture, and forged ironwork.

Barnes Foundation

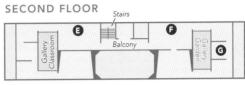

SECOND FLOOR

Stairs

E   **F**

Gallery Classroom   Balcony   Gallery Garden   **G**

COLLECTIONS GALLERY

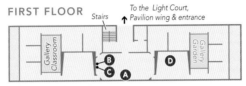

FIRST FLOOR

Stairs

To the Light Court, ↑ Pavilion wing & entrance

Gallery Classroom   **B** **C** **A**   **D**   Gallery Garden

COLLECTIONS GALLERY

Surrounded by exhibition spaces and a large atrium, the core of the new building was carefully constructed to mimic precisely the rooms of the original location, a layout in which Barnes had personally arranged his eclectic montages of fine art and everyday objects. Matisse painted the mural **A** *The Dance II* to fit precisely beneath the (reconstructed) arches of the large main room above **B** *Card Players,* one of Cézanne's favorite subjects, and **C** *Models,* Seurat's (1859–1891) study for Ile de la Grande Jatte. Among notable works in other rooms: Van Gogh's

D *Postman,* a portrait of the artist's mailman Joseph Roulin; **E** *Scout Attacked by a Tiger,* one of Rousseau's (1844–1910) signature jungle scenes; and Picasso's paternal, symbolist painting **F** *Harlequins.* Among the objets, don't miss **G** *Seated Couple,* one of Barnes's 200 African sculptures. ⏱ *3 hrs. 2025 Benjamin Franklin Pkwy.* ☎ *215/278-7000. www. barnesfoundation.org. Reservations highly recommended, well in advance. Admission starts at $18 adults, $15 seniors; parking $15. Wed–Thurs & Sat–Mon 10am–6pm; Fri 10am–10pm.*

9 ★★★ **Rodin Museum.** Nearby up the Parkway, this hidden gem of a museum houses the largest collection of works by Pierre August Rodin (1840–1917) outside the Musée Rodin in Paris. You'll recognize the artist's iconic works such as *The Thinker* and the *Gates of*

Hell, but don't miss the smaller, more process-oriented exhibits of bronze castings, plaster studies, original sketchbooks, letters, and books. ⏱ *1 hr. 2151 Ben Franklin Pkwy. (at 22nd St.)* ☎ *215/763-8100. Suggested admission $8 adults, $7 seniors, $6 students (or get $20 Art*

Museum complex ticket). www.rodin museum.org. Wed–Mon 10am–5pm.

⑩ ★ Washington Monument. Alike in name alone to the capitol city's famed obelisk, this fountain no longer spouts water but does represent the entry to the Philadelphia Museum of Art. Little-known sculptor Rudolf Siemering (1835–1905) completed the work in 1897. A proud General Washington, in tricorn hat and cape, and mounted on a tall steed, once stood at the entrance to Fairmount Park. Today, he faces City Hall, inside Eakins Oval, named for the beloved Philadelphia painter. ⏰ *15 min. Eakins Oval (26th St. & Ben Franklin Pkwy.).*

⑪ ★★ Philadelphia Museum of Art. This Greco-Roman temple on a hill has 227,000 works for your not-so-quick perusal. Among the masterpieces: Cézanne's (1839–1906) monumental *Bathers*; regionally themed works by Eakins; classics from Van Gogh (1853–1890), Rubens (1577–1640), Duchamp (1877–1968), and Monet (1840–1926); plus, stunning collections of furniture, jewelry, ceramics, and armor. The permanent installations of a medieval cloister and a Japanese teahouse are especially restful and lovely. ⏰ *2 hrs. (For more information, see p 13.) 26th St. & Ben Franklin Pkwy.*

⑫ ★★ Perelman Building. This recently opened, thoroughly gorgeous Art Deco building just across the street also belongs to the PMA. The Perelman offers marvelously tactile collections in textile and design, along with special exhibits in the same realms; has a distinguished art reference library; and serves as a satellite for museum exhibits, including Andrew Wyeth (1917–2009), Matisse (1869–1954), and Renoir (1841–1919). Until the planned Frank Gehry–designed (b. 1929) tunnel connects this building to the PMA, a shuttle operates between them. ⏰ *1 hr. Fairmount & Pennsylvania aves. ☎ 215/763-8100. www.philamuseum.org. Admission on same ticket as Art Museum. Tues–Sun 10am–5pm.*

The Perelman Building offers collections of textiles and design.

The Best Special-Interest Tours

Philly with Kids

Map Legend
- Ⓜ SEPTA Subway
- Ⓟ PATCO Light Rail
- † Church
- ✡ Synagogue
- ▪ Point of Interest

To inset

1 Dutch Eating Place
2 Please Touch Museum
3 Franklin Square
4 Square Burger
5 Ride the Ducks
6 Storyteller benches
7 Franklin Court
8 Franklin Fountain
9 Betsy Ross House
10 Elfreth's Alley
11 Liberty 360

In a big city that feels small, small people feel big. A fuss-free day of the kid-centric calls for frequent breaks, comfortable footwear, and knowing which activities to save for another day, such as the Philadelphia Zoo (see p 45, bullet ❷), Adventure Aquarium (see p 96, bullet ❻), and Franklin Institute (see p 47, bullet ❺). Even without these three biggies, there's still a great day's worth of fun to be had for little people in the City of Brotherly Love. START: **Please Touch Museum, 4231 Ave. of the Republic.**

The Please Touch Museum features a circa-1824 carousel.

1 ★★ **Dutch Eating Place.** An optional pre-tour fueling stop. If you want to dig into the biggest, best breakfast in all of Philly—blueberry pancakes, apple toast, and oddly yummy scrapple (PA's meat-scrap specialty)—grab a counter seat at this Mennonite-run luncheonette in bustling Reading Terminal Market. (Coffee-loving parents can also make a pit-stop at Old City Coffee's nearby kiosk.) *12th & Arch sts.* ☎ *215/922-0425. Closed Sun. $.*

2 ★★ **Please Touch Museum.** Take the purple PHLASH bus (see p 161) out to Fairmount Park's Memorial Hall. Here, at the serious-looking site of the 1876 Centennial Exhibition (a.k.a. the first World's Fair) is Philly's least-serious of museums, a bright, educational mega-playground for the Gymboree set. As its name suggests, the Please Touch's number-one rule is opposite of that of most museums. Climbing, throwing, splashing, honking, jumping, riding, and playing are actively encouraged. Little ones will love the waist-high water tables of River Adventure, the faux shopping at a low-shelved supermarket, the "work" of a safety-first construction zone, a magically rendered Alice in Wonderland maze, regular story times, and a mint-condition circa-1824 carousel. Philly-inspired exhibits of a once-beloved kids' TV show, *Captain Noah*, and the monorail from the old toy

Franklin Square dates to 1682 and has recently added child-friendly attractions like mini-golf.

department of the historic John Wanamaker store offer a glimpse of local childhoods of yore. There's also a busy cafe for juice and pizza. The staff is marvelous, but they are not babysitters. Guardians must accompany children at all times. ⏱ *2 hr. 4231 Ave. of the Republic.* ☎ *215/581-3181. www.pleasetouch museum.org. Admission $16 (free for children 1 & under). Mon–Sat 9am–5pm; Sun 11am–5pm.*

❸ ★★★ **Franklin Square.** One of William Penn's five original squares, this 7½-acre plot dates to 1682 and has recently been reincarnated as a low-key, amusement park–like haven for families. Among the attractions: an 18-hole, Philadelphia-theme mini-golf; a slew of jungle gyms for all ages; a giant sand sculpture; an excellent carousel; an 1838 basin fountain; and benches where "Once Upon A Nation" performers tell entertaining historical stories and make balloon animals. ⏱ *1½ hr. Btw. 6th & 7th sts. on Race St. www.historic philadelphia.org. Carousel: $2.50. Mini-golf: $9 adults, $7 children 3–12. Apr 1–Oct 31 daily 10am–9pm (to 10pm Fri–Sat).*

❹ ★★ **Square Burger.** Stephen Starr, Philly's biggest-deal restaurateur, is responsible for the inexpensive and delicious hamburgers, salami-wrapped kosher hotdogs, hand-cut fries, and milkshakes made with Tastykake Butterscotch

The amphibious Ride the Ducks vehicles provide a kid-friendly environment for touring Old City and Society Hill.

Krimpets (a local, er, delicacy) at this walk-up stand—named, alas, for the location (Franklin Square), not the shape of the burgers. *200 S. 6th St. (btw. 6th & 7th sts. on Race St.)* ☎ *215/629-4026. $.*

⑤ ★★ **Ride the Ducks.** One of the best things about exploring with kids is getting to act like a kid yourself. On these land-to-water touring vehicles, delightfully immature behavior is practically de rigueur. Though you won't get the most erudite rundown of local history, you will see a nice bit of Old City and Society Hill, make ridiculous noises with plastic "duckbills," and giggle at the joke-cracking, oldies-blaring guides. If your child is brave enough to take the wheel once you reach the Delaware River, it'll be the highlight of his or her day. ① *1½ hr. Independence Visitor Center, 6th & Market sts.* ☎ *877/887-8225. www. phillyducks.com. Admission $27 adults, $17 children 4–12.*

⑥ ★★ **Storyteller benches.** At benches scattered throughout the Independence Mall—especially between 3rd and 6th Street and Chestnut and Walnut, costumed "Once Upon a Nation's" characters engage all ages in tales of Colonial life. ① *30 min. Chestnut St. btw. 3rd & 4th sts. www.historicphiladelphia. org. Free admission. Memorial Day to Labor Day 11am–4pm (days vary).*

⑦ ★★ **Franklin Court.** Beyond an unassuming brick archway on Market Street is the site, if not the structure, of Ben Franklin's Philadelphia home. The original dwelling was razed in 1812. All that's left is an archeological dig–looking foundation and the modern steel frame "ghost" girder meant to represent the original house—neither of which might impress the kids. What they will love are the Benjamin Franklin Life & Legacy Museum—completely renovated in 2012-13—that cleverly outlines Franklin's irrepressible ingenuity and the Colonials that seem to live and

"Once Upon a Nation" storytellers and re-enactors bring the Colonial era to life throughout Philly.

work around the court. In the museum: Some of Franklin's lesser-known, more offbeat inventions, such as bowls for a glass armonica (played like water glasses at the dinner table) and swim fins (Franklin was a champion swimmer). Better yet are the storytellers (even "Ben" appears regularly beneath his beloved mulberry tree) to enliven the court with true tales and craft projects. The gift shop here is especially nice; have the kids buy a postcard and get the instant satisfaction they crave by mailing it at the still-active post office where Franklin served as the nation's first Postmaster General, and where all mail is still hand-cancelled. (It's the only post office in the U.S. that does not fly an American flag—since none existed when it first opened in 1775). ⏱ 1½ hr. 314–322 Market St. ☎ 215/965-2305. www.nps.gov/inde. Free admission. Daily 11am–5pm. Post office closed Sun.

The tiny Betsy Ross House recreates the life of an average Colonial family.

floats, milkshakes, and more at this purposefully old-fashioned soda fountain (est. 2004). 116 Market St. ☎ 215/627-1899. www.franklinfountain.com. $.

⑧ ★★★ Franklin Fountain. Homemade ice cream in flavors both familiar (vanilla bean, mint chip, peach) and throwback (teaberry gum, licorice) come by the scoop in parfaits, banana splits,

⑨ ★ Betsy Ross House. Flag-making lore aside, this tiny house seems just the right fit for pint-sized explorers, who'll marvel at the absolute compactness of life for the average Colonial family. Although

Old-fashioned Franklin Fountain boasts several varieties of homemade ice cream.

Come An' Play

Up I-95 about 27 miles (43.4km), Sesame Place (100 Sesame Rd., Langhorne; ☎ 866/GO-4-ELMO [866/464-3566]; www.sesame place.com; $61 adults and children 2 and over [$41 after 3pm]; combo ticket with Please Touch Museum $64; daily Memorial Day–Labor Day [and most weekends out of season]; hours vary wildly, from 10am to anywhere from 6 to 9pm) is theme-park paradise for the post-toddler set. The 14-acre outdoor "neighborhood" of recreation—and nothing but recreation—offers a dizzying array of splashy water park-style rides (bring bathing suits), kiddie coasters, a carousel, and hundreds of ways to experience Elmo and his ilk, including a twice-daily parade and regular staged performances. The park is consistently crowded, so arrive early.

Quaker seamstress Elizabeth (Betsy) Ross may not have even lived here, the house's preservers sure have made it look like she did, what with careful placement of reusable ivory tablets, pinecones to help start hearth fires, and a handy kitchen hourglass. The courtyard park separating the house from the street isn't just the burial ground for Ross and her last husband—it's the place where you're most likely to meet "Betsy" herself, and to hear her stories. (See p 11, bullet **9**.) ⏱ *30 min. 239 Arch St. www.historic philadelphia.org. Free admission.*

⑩ ★★★ Elfreth's Alley. No need to do the full tour of the museum at the oldest continuously inhabited street in the United States. It's enough to walk down this narrow cobblestone stretch, look up at the centuries-old row houses, think with your child of your own dwelling, and offer a gentle lesson about getting along with the neighbors. (See p 51, bullet **4**.) ⏱ *20 min. Off 2nd St., toward Front St., btw. Arch & Race sts.*

⑪ Liberty 360. A Hall-of-Presidents-type exhibit for the 21st century: a 3-D, 360-degree film in

which Ben Franklin takes you through early American history with a focus on the symbols and icons of Americana (bald eagle, State of Liberty and, naturally, the Liberty Bell that sits across the street). ⏱ *20 min. PECO Energy Center, 6th & Chestnut sts. ☎ 877/426-1776. www.historicphiladelphia.org. Admission $6 adults, $5 students, seniors & children, or $20 for a family of 4. Hours vary, but mostly daily 10am–6pm (to 8pm Mon-Sat June 24–Aug 10; to 3pm Sun Sept–Mar).*

Liberty 360 3-D uses 21st-century tech to tell tales of the Revolutionary era.

What Would Rocky Do?

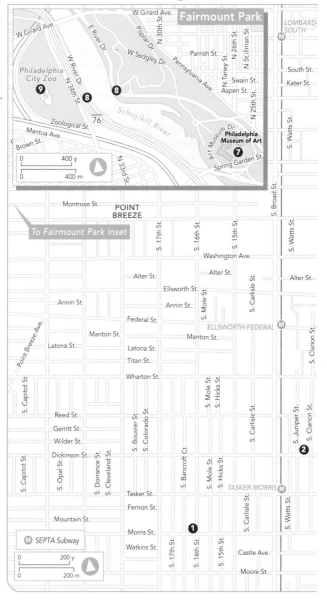

1. St. Thomas Aquinas Church
2. Victor Café
3. Pat's King of Steaks
4. Italian Market
5. Sarcone's Deli
6. Palumbo Playground
7. Philadelphia Museum of Art Steps
8. Kelly and MLK Jr. drives
9. Philadelphia Zoo

In 1976, a rags-to-riches film about a hardscrabble pugilist from Philly's Kensington neighborhood captured America's heart—and, as far as Philadelphians are concerned, never let go. Below are highlights of Rocky Balboa's favorite spots. (One tip: Don't attempt a literal version of the "Rocky Run." You'll be dashing across town for days.) START: **17th & Morris Sts—in South Philly, yo.**

The Italian Market is America's oldest outdoor market.

❶ ★ St. Thomas Aquinas Church. The little parish where Rocky and Adrian got hitched isn't exactly set up to host tourists, but you can pop in for a look-see. The gilded, chandeliered, Italian baroque-style 1904 St. Thomas has been called the loveliest Catholic Church in South Philadelphia. ⏱ ½ hr. 1719 Morris St. (at 17th St.) ☎ 215/334-2312. www.staquinas. com. Free admission.

❷ Victor Café. This South Philly, restaurant famous for its opera-singing waiters, served as the retired champ's restaurant, "Adrian's," in 2006's *Rocky Balboa. 1303 Dickinson St. (btw. Broad & 13th sts.).* ☎ *215/468-3040. www.victor cafe.com.*

❸ ★★ Pat's King of Steaks. Balboa started his day with a glass of raw eggs. Only slightly less off-putting is a breakfast of bread-swaddled steak topped "wid" fried onions and "Whiz." But, heck; if you're gonna do it once in your life, do it where, in 1930, a hot-dog seller invented Philly's most famous sandwich—and 46 years later, Rocky ate one. ⏱ ½ hr. 1237 E. Passyunk Ave. (at Wharton St.). ☎ 215/468-1546. www.pats kingofsteaks.com. Open 24 hrs.

❹ ★★ Italian Market. America's oldest outdoor market apparently welcomes odd guys in gray sweats who run in traffic. Filmed here: The scene where a vendor—who had no idea a movie was being filmed—tosses Balboa an orange. How the boxer ate the fruit while jogging past flaming 55-gallon drums of trash is anyone's guess. Our advice: Don't run. Stroll. Shop. ⏱ 2 hr. S 9th St., btw. Christian & Federal sts. www.9thstreetitalianmarket.com. (See p 18, bullet ⓫.)

5 ★★ **Sarcone's Deli.** Amazing hoagies loaded up with prosciutto, capicola, hard salami, sharp provolone, roasted red peppers, even broccoli rabe, served on Italian bread baked at the family's circa-1918 bakery. *734 S. 9th St. (at Fitzwater St.)* ☎ *215/922-1717. www.sarconesdeli.com. $.*

6 **kids Palumbo Playground.** There's no proof Stallone ever set foot in this South Philly neighborhood park, but it's a great spot for the kids to enjoy the jungle gym and swing set, and for you to engage in a few exercises without having to punch a frozen side of beef. Squat thrusts, anyone? ⏱ *½ hr. Btw. 9th & 10th sts., Fitzwater & Bainbridge sts.*

7 ★★ **kids Philadelphia Museum of Art Steps.** If you don't know what happened here, consider re-renting the movie. The scene of Balboa running up the 72 steps, turning around, and pumping his fists in the air was an instant American film classic (and one of the first scenes filmed with a Steadicam, invented by Philly boy Garrett Brown). Each year, thousands of visitors decide they're "Gonna Fly Now" (many never set foot in the museum itself). At the top of the steps is a bronze imprint of Stallone's Converse sneakers. At the foot of the steps (to the north), a Rocky statue. ⏱ *½ hr. (See p 13, bullet ②).*

8 ★★ **Kelly and MLK Jr. drives.** Stretching from the Art Museum along opposing sides of the Schuylkill River, these winding roads are each paralleled by a wide, sculpture-studded, tree-lined pedestrian path. It's a handsome spot, as crew teams skim along the river. It's also your best bet for attempting a Rocky-like run. A loop from the Art Museum over Strawberry Mansion Bridge and back is 6¼ miles. ⏱ *1½ hr.*

9 ★★ **kids Philadelphia Zoo.** The country's first zoo dates back to 1874 and consists of 42 acres on the west side of Fairmount Park. More than 1,300 animals dwell here. A few not-to-be-missed spots: The new McNeil Avian Center, with walk-through junglelike habitats, a 4-D Migration Theater, and extinct-in-the-wild Guam Rail and Micronesian Kingfisher; Carnivore Kingdom's snow leopards, red pandas, and family of giant otters; and African Plains for warthogs, antelope, gazelles, giraffes, hippos, and zebras. There's also a petting zoo and, for an extra fee, a ride 400 feet above the city via the tiger-striped Zooballoon. Best bet for transportation: Take a PHLASH or SEPTA bus, since parking is sparse and traffic gets heavy. (As for the Rocky connection: In *Rocky II*, our hero proposed to his sweetheart Adrian, played by Talia Shire, on a winter's day at what is now Big Cat Falls.) ⏱ *2 hrs. 34th St. & Girard Ave.* ☎ *215/243-1100. www.philadelphiazoo.org. Admission $20 adults, $18 children 2–11. Zooballoon additional $15. Mar–Oct daily 9:30am–5pm; Nov–Feb daily 9:30am–4pm.*

The Rocky statue.

Romantic Philadelphia

M	SEPTA Subway	
P	PATCO Light Rail	
T	Trolley	
†	Church	

1 Love Park
2 Parc
3 Rittenhouse Square
4 Mütter Museum
5 Franklin Institute
6 Fountain Restaurant
7 Rodin Museum
8 Eastern State Penitentiary
9 Mercury Pavilion

Touring Philly à deux can be twice the fun—provided you know where to go. Lucky for couples, Center City's laid-back sidewalks are wide enough for ample hand-holding, and its park benches were custom made for snuggling. (It didn't earn the name "City of Brotherly Love" for nothing.) START: **JFK Plaza, JFK Blvd btw 15th & 16th St.**

1 ★★ **Love Park.** If you haven't felt compelled to say those three little words yet, you'll certainly feel the mood when you take a seat in this charming urban park, where you won't be able to miss Robert Indiana's bright red, font-based LOVE sculpture. (If that's not a sign, nothing is.) ⏱ ½ hr. *15th St. & JFK Blvd.*

2 ★★ **Parc.** Come nighttime, this glittery Parisian brasserie absolutely bursts with the see-and-be-seen crowd. At breakfast, however, the light is naturally dim and the vibe is delightfully low-key. Order a smoked salmon tartine, polenta and eggs Basquaise, or a pain au chocolat—and linger. 228 S. *18th St. (at Locust St.)* ☎ *215/545-2262. www.parc-restaurant.com.* $$.

3 ★★ **Rittenhouse Square.** Designed by French architect Paul Philippe Cret in 1913, this park is the leafy heart of Philly's fanciest neighborhood. Start your day here, when the grass is dewy and everyone else is rushing off to work. ⏱ ½ hr. *Btw. 18th & 19th sts., Walnut & Rittenhouse sts.*

4 ★★ **Mutter Museum.** You know how, at scary scenes in horror flicks, she will reach over and grab your arm for comfort—even bury her face in your chest so as not to watch? Well, this 19th-century museum of odd and macabre medical mishaps is like walking through a Victorian horror movie. It is intensely, fascinatingly creepy, and

This bright red statue is the centerpiece of Love Park.

possibly not suited for every Romantic. Goth couples, on the other hand, frequently rent it out for weddings. Not kidding. (See p 64 [Neighborhood Tours: Rittenhouse]) ⏱ 1 hr. *19 S. 22nd St. (btw. Market & Chestnut sts.).* ☎ *215/ 563-3737, ext 293. www.collphyphil. org.* Admission $15 adults, $13 seniors & military with ID, $10 students, free 5 and under. Daily 10am–5pm.

5 ★★★ **Franklin Institute.** Although this science museum is a bit kids-centric, it also boasts arguably the weirdest spot in town to steal a kiss, a giant-but-cramped, continuously beating, walk-through heart. If that doesn't work, there's also the drama of an IMAX theater (additional fee to enter) for innocuous cuddling, the 1810 Maillardet automaton that inspired Hugo, and

The giant walk-through heart at the Franklin Institute.

interactive exhibits that feel straight out of a one-on-one date on *The Bachelor,* where you get to test the laws of physics through a variety of adrenaline activities. Too sporty? Come back at night to peer deep into the universe through the rooftop telescopes. ① *2 hr. 20th St. & Ben Franklin Pkwy.* ☎ *215/448-1200. www.fi.edu. Admission $17 adults, $13 children 4–11; additional $6 adults for IMAX Theater. Daily 9:30am–5pm (some summer days til 7pm).*

⑥ ★★★ Fountain Restaurant. The classic, romantic place to drop a fortune on lunch, in the elegant Four Seasons hotel. *1 Logan Sq. (at 18th St.).* ☎ *215/963-1500. www. fourseasons.com/philadelphia. $$$.*

⑦ ★★★ Rodin Museum. Is there an artist more romantic than Auguste Rodin (1840–1917)? Perhaps, but there's not a Philadelphia art museum more romantic than this petite space, with its leafy overhangs and serene sculpture. Plus, if you recently bought, say, a circular piece of diamond jewelry, you won't be put off by the admission, a suggested donation of $5. (See p 15, bullet ⑤). ① *1 hr. 22nd St. & Ben Franklin Pkwy.*

⑧ ★★ Eastern State Penitentiary. Back when it opened in 1829, a visit to this medieval fortress–looking prison was no fun at all. These days, however, a stroll through Eastern State's decrepit cell blocks is perversely beautiful. An hour-long audio tour offers a glimpse into solitary confinement "rehabilitation" cells (in use until 1971) and into the lives of its inmates, including robber Willie Sutton (1901–1980), gangster Al Capone (1899–1947), and one very naughty dog. The weeks leading up to Halloween, ESP hosts the city's scariest haunted house—a perfect excuse for some extended hand-holding. ① *1 hr. 2027 Fairmount Ave. (btw. 21 & 22 sts.).* ☎ *215/236-3300. www.easternstate.org. Admission $14 adults, $12 seniors, $10 students and children (not recommended for children under 7). Daily 10am–5pm.*

⑨ ★★ Mercury Pavilion. Got a ring in your pocket? Keep it there until you reach this cliff-top overlook between the Philadelphia Museum of Art and the Waterworks/Boathouse Row, the prettiest neoclassical gazebo in town for watching a sunset and declaring your undying affection. ① *Whatever it takes. Behind Philadelphia Museum of Art (see p 13).* ●

Old City

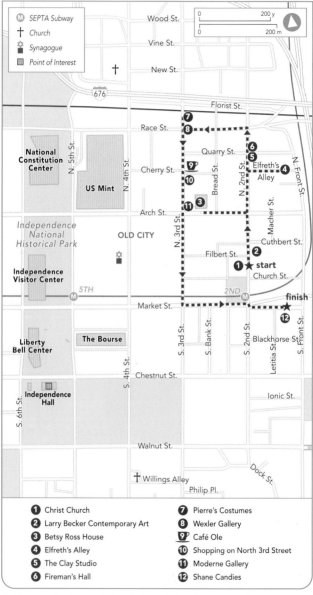

Map legend:
- Ⓜ SEPTA Subway
- † Church
- ✡ Synagogue
- ▢ Point of Interest

Streets and locations shown on map:
Wood St., Vine St., New St., Florist St., Race St., Quarry St., Cherry St., Arch St., Filbert St., Church St., Cuthbert St., Macher St., Market St., Blackhorse St., Chestnut St., Ionic St., Walnut St., Willings Alley, Philip Pl., Dock St.

N. 5th St., N. 4th St., N. 3rd St., N. 2nd St., N. Front St., Bread St., S. 3rd St., S. Bank St., S. 2nd St., Letitia St., S. Front St., S. 4th St., S. 6th St.

National Constitution Center, US Mint, Independence National Historical Park, OLD CITY, Independence Visitor Center, Liberty Bell Center, The Bourse, Independence Hall

676

5TH, 2ND

start, finish

1 Christ Church
2 Larry Becker Contemporary Art
3 Betsy Ross House
4 Elfreth's Alley
5 The Clay Studio
6 Fireman's Hall
7 Pierre's Costumes
8 Wexler Gallery
9 Café Ole
10 Shopping on North 3rd Street
11 Moderne Gallery
12 Shane Candies

Previous page: Students stroll along the Locust Walk at the University of Pennsylvania.

The tree-lined streets of Philadelphia's most landmark-laden neighborhood are perfect for exploring by foot. What's loveliest about Old City is the seamless urban melding of old and new, Colonial and contemporary, classical and artful, and the excellent (and often eccentric) discoveries that pop up where you least expect them. START: **Old City Coffee, 221 Church St.**

❶ ★★ **Christ Church.** To Old City residents, the gleaming white spire of this most colonial of churches is as iconic to their neighborhood as City Hall's statue of William Penn (1644–1718) is to the whole of Philadelphia. A few facts worth noting about this built-in-1727–1754 but-still-well-attended-today landmark: The massive Palladian window behind the altar was the inspiration for that of Independence Hall. Assigned seating was by pew rather than open benches (note Washington's [1732–1799] spot). William Penn was baptized in the font, a gift from All Hallows' Church in London. It's perfectly fine to walk on the floor-level tomb markers in the nave. And the shaded churchyard benches are great places to catch up on your people watching. (See p 27, ❶.) 🕐 ½ hr. 2nd & Market sts. Free admission.

❷ ★ **Larry Becker Contemporary Art.** Your first example of the newer half of Old City, this minimalist, modern gallery displays the mostly spare and always modern work of international artists such as Robert Ryman (b. 1930), Rebecca Salter (b. 1977), and native son Quentin Morris (b. 1945). 🕐 20 min. 43 N. 2nd St. ☎ 215/925-5389. Free admission. By appointment only.

❸ ★ kids **Betsy Ross House.** Another architectural emblem, this American seamstress' apparent dwelling is a brilliant example of the absolute compactness of life for the average Colonial family. Elizabeth (Betsy) Ross (1752–1836) was a

Mass at the 18th-century Christ Church is still well attended.

Quaker needlewoman who, newly widowed in 1776, worked as a seamstress and upholsterer out of the space that is now the gift shop. According to lore, General Washington asked Ross to sew the original flag, 13 stars set in a field of 13 red and white stripes. According to recorded history, Ross at the very least sewed such flags for the American fleet. A courtyard park separates the house from the street; here Ross and her last husband are buried. (See p 11, ❾.) 🕐 ½ hr. Free admission. 239 Arch St.

❹ ★★ **Elfreth's Alley.** From a small house to a small street of small houses. In 1700, this cobblestone lane was the address of a melting pot of artisans and tradesmen who worked in shipping. Fifty years later, the street was occupied by haberdashers, bakers, printers, and carpenters. In the late 18th through 19th centuries, Jewish, African-American, Welsh, and German residents lived along Elfreth's Alley. Number 126, the circa-1755 Mantua (cape) Maker's House belonged to blacksmith Jeremiah Elfreth (1723–1765). It's now the street's museum, with a restored back garden and an interior that includes a dressmaker's shop and bedroom. Best time to visit: The second weekend in June, when most of the alley's houses are open for touring. (See p 11, **10**.) ⓘ *1 hr. Off 2nd St., toward Front St., btw. Arch & Race sts.* ☎ *215/574-0560. www.elfrethsalley.org. Free admission to visitor center & gift shop; Museum: $5 adults, $2 children 6–12, free 5 & under (includes 20-minute tour). For tour schedule, call or check Twitter (@elfrethsalley); museum open Tues–Sat 10am–5pm, Sun noon–5pm.*

5 ★ **The Clay Studio.** This center for ceramics is one of the busiest artist spaces in this always-busy artist community. The Studio—which started as just that, an affordable workspace—now includes a two-floor gallery for new exhibits by international and up-and-coming ceramicists. Workshops and classrooms offer a behind-the-scenes look. ⓘ *20 min. 137–139 N. 2nd St. (btw. Arch & Race sts.).* ☎ *215/925-3453. www.theclay studio.org. Free admission.*

6 **kids** **Fireman's Hall.** Run by the Philadelphia Fire Department, this restored 1902 firehouse traces its history back to Ben Franklin (1706–1790), the country's first fire marshal. On display: A circa-1730 hand pumper, the nation's oldest steam fire engine, modern-day fire safety displays, and artifacts from Ground Zero. ⓘ *½ hr. 147 N. 2nd St.* ☎ *215/923-1438. www.firemans hall.org. Free admission. Tues–Sat 10am–4:30pm.*

7 **kids** **Pierre's Costumes.** More than a million costumes reside at this spot under the Ben Franklin Bridge, a truly fun place to browse—or, if the occasion calls for it, to buy an Uncle Sam top hat, George Washington wig, or just about any Halloween outfit imaginable. ⓘ *20 min. 211 N. 3rd St.* ☎ *215/925-7121. www.costumers.*

The restored 1902 Fireman's Hall.

Wexler Gallery hosts a variety of cutting-edge exhibits.

com. Mon–Fri 10am–5:30pm, Sat 10am–4pm.

8 ★ Wexler Gallery. This serene corner space hosts a marvelous variety of cutting-edge art exhibits of fine crafts, exquisite furniture, art glass, studio jewelry, and more. Like most of the galleries in Old City, Wexler stays open late to welcome art-fueled revelers on the first Friday of each month. ⏱ ½ hr. *201 N. 3rd St. (at Race St.).* ☎ *215/ 923-7030. www.wexlergallery.com. Free admission. Tues–Sat 10am–6pm.*

9 Café Ole. If you haven't yet noticed why Old City has earned its nickname, the "Hipstoric District," you will once you set foot in this laid-back cafe. Stand in line for truly cool fresh-mint iced tea, creative grilled panini, and tasty hummus plates and Mediterranean salads that won't break the bank. *147 N. 3rd St.* ☎ *215/627-2140. $.*

10 ★★ Shopping. We may be pointing out the obvious, but this stretch of North 3rd Street between Race and Market streets is sublimely studded with great boutiques—and the occasional bargain. Read more about what's in stores in Chapter 4 (see p 73) or just take our word for it and pop into Sugarcube, Art in the Age, Vagabond, Third Street Habit, Reward, Lost & Found—or whatever latest vintage or new shop may catch your eye. (We promise you'll come out dressed like you totally belong in the Hipstoric District.) ⏱ *Take all the time you need.*

11 ★ Moderne Gallery. Among the handful of really great furnishings shops in this area is Bob Aibel's 20,000-square-foot space, gently stocked with decorative arts from the last century. Look for rare French Art Deco, vintage George Nakashima (1905–1990), Wharton Esherick (1887–1970) pieces, and more artistic gems, all on display and for sale. ⏱ ½ hr. *111 N. 3rd St.* ☎ *215/923-8536. www.moderne gallery.com. Free admission.*

12 ★ kids Shane Candies. Anyone want to taste history in the country's oldest candy store? For 99 years, the Shane family stocked their shop with their famous buttercreams, almond butter crunch, cherry bark, and confections galore; a few years ago they passed the legacy onto the Berley brothers (who run Franklin Fountain a few doors up; see p 40). ⏱ *20 min. 110 Market St.* ☎ *215/922-1048. www. shanecandies.com.*

Society Hill

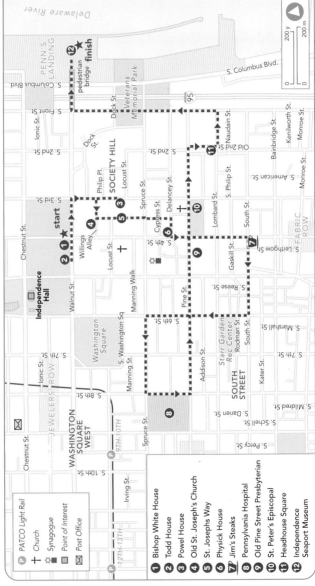

Delaware River

PENN'S LANDING

★ pedestrian bridge finish

S. Columbus Blvd.

Veterans Memorial Park

SOCIETY HILL

start

Independence Hall

Washington Square

WASHINGTON SQUARE WEST

JEWELERS' ROW

SOUTH STREET

FABRIC ROW

Legend:
- (P) PATCO Light Rail
- ✝ Church
- ✡ Synagogue
- ■ Point of Interest
- ⊠ Post Office

1. Bishop White House
2. Todd House
3. Powel House
4. Old St. Joseph's Church
5. St. Josephs Way
6. Physick House
7. Jim's Steaks
8. Pennsylvania Hospital
9. Old Pine Street Presbyterian
10. St. Peter's Episcopal
11. Headhouse Square
12. Independence Seaport Museum

200 y / 200 m

Society Hill has the largest concentration of 18th– and early-19th-century architecture in the city—and the country. It also has some of Philly's most modern houses, intended at one point to improve the caliber of the neighborhood. Loosely bound by Walnut and South streets, the river, and 8th Street, the neighborhood gets its name from the Free Society of Traders, a wealthy 18th-century group of Quaker financiers who footed some of William Penn's bills. As you explore, keep an eye out for details such as "busybody" mirrors in upper-floor windows, invented by Ben Franklin and used by residents to see who's at the door without having to descend the stairs; original wrought-iron boot scrapers; and sidewalks that bear antique hitching posts and marble steps, relics of horse-and-buggy days. Before you go, pick up tickets for the first two stops at the Independence Visitor Center (see p 9, ❶). START: **3rd & Walnut sts.**

❶ ★★ **Bishop White House.** This elegant circa-1786 home exemplifies gracious upper-class life in early America. Owner William White was quite a worldly fellow: Notice his library, with Encyclopedia Britannica, Sir Walter Scott's novels, the Koran—and, a luxury for any reader, an indoor "necessary." ⏱ *½ hr. (See p 26, ⓭.)*

❷ ★ **Todd House.** A much more modest (but far from small) dwelling belonged to John Todd, Jr. This solid, circa-1775 Georgian had a Colonial version of the family storefront, with a first-floor office and a large upstairs parlor, where Todd's widow Dolley (1768–1849) is said to have met one Mr. James Madison (1751–1836). ⏱ *½ hr. (See p 26, ⓮.)*

❸ ★★ **Powel House.** Built in 1765 by a wealthy merchant, this gorgeous Colonial Georgian became the home of Philadelphia mayor Samuel Powel (1738–1793) and his wife, Elizabeth Willing (1743–1830), in 1769. The gentle couple were major party throwers: Anyone who was anyone—Lafayette

Physick House was home to "the father of American surgery."

(1757–1834), Washington, Rush (1756–1833), Franklin—feasted and danced here. (Adams [1735–1826] dubbed the Powels' parties "sinful dinners.") Note the entryway's bas-relief plasterwork, mahogany wainscoting, ballroom chandelier, and formal garden. Since the house is still available for private parties, call before visiting. ⓘ ½ hr. 244 S. 3rd St. (btw. Walnut & Locust sts). ☎ 215/627-0364. www.philalandmarks.org. Admission $5 adults, $4 seniors & students; $12 families. Tours Thurs–Sat noon–4pm; Sun 1–4pm (Jan–Feb by appointment only).

④ ★ Old St. Joseph's Church. Double back up 3rd and turn left down Willings Alley to this church, which was founded in 1733 and was the only place in the English-speaking world where Roman Catholics—such as Revolutionary hero General Lafayette—could celebrate Mass publicly (see p 25). ⓘ 15 min. 321 Willings Alley (4th St., near Walnut St.). ☎ 215/923-1733. www.oldstjoseph.org. Free admission.

⑤ St. Josephs Way. Walk between the buildings directly across from Old St. Joe's to enter Bingham Court, a collection of rectilinear brick-and-glass townhouses designed by I. M. Pei as part of a 1960s Society Hill redevelopment initiative; they now go for around $1 million. Continue south along St. Josephs Way, part of a network of narrow alleys between 3rd and 4th streets. Turn right onto Delancey Street (after popping into Delancey Park to pat its iconic three bears). ⓘ 15 min.

⑥ ★ Physick House. Freestanding, with a walled garden, this home diverges from its conjoined peers. Madeira wine importer Henry Hill built the place in 1786; subsequent owner Philip Syng Physick (1768–1837) added Federal flourishes, an inkstand (with Ben

The azalea gardens of Pennsylvania Hospital, the first hospital in the American Colonies.

Franklin's fingerprints), and 18th century Italian art. Known as "the father of American surgery," Physick invented the stomach pump, created new ways to repair fractures, designed needle forceps, pioneered catgut sutures, removed thousands of bladder stones from Supreme Court Chief Justice John Marshall (1755–1835), was doctor to Dolley Madison and Andrew Jackson (1767–1845)—oh, and he helped invent soda, too. ⓘ 40 min. 321 S. 4th St. (at Delancey St.). ☎ 215/925-7866. www.philalandmarks.org. Admission $5 adults, $4 seniors & students. Thurs–Sat noon–4pm; Sun 1–4pm (Jan–Feb by appointment only).

⑦ ★ Jim's Steaks. If it's past 11am, there's a line at this corner steak stand, a pioneer in the field of cheesesteaks since 1939. To enjoy the real deal, order "wit (onions)

and (Cheez) Whiz" (or, if you must, provolone). Bonus: Unlike its competitors, Jim's serves beer. *4th & South sts.* ☎ *215/928-1911. www. jimssteaks.com. $.*

8 ★ Pennsylvania Hospital.
The Colonies' first hospital was founded by—you guessed it—one Benjamin Franklin (along with Dr. Thomas Bond). Back in 1751, it seemed to its contemporaries like a strange venture in social welfare. Today, it's as vibrant as ever—and welcomes visitors to tour its historic sections. The hospital consists of two wings connected by a grand Center Building, the highlight of which was a sky-lit surgical amphitheater of 1804. As you might imagine, the hospital's interiors have much altered since those days, but the lovely azalea garden (facing Pine St.) remains, as does a carefully tended apothecary garden of medicinal herbs and an 1817 Benjamin West painting of *Christ Healing the Sick in the Temple.* ○ *½ hr. 800 Spruce St. (at 8th)* ☎ *215/829-3000. www.pennhealth.com/pahosp. Free admission; tours available if you book 48 hours ahead. Mon–Fri 8:30am–4:30pm.*

9 ★ Old Pine Street Presbyterian. When John Adams wasn't grumbling about fancy parties, he might have been sitting in a pew inside the city's oldest standing (ca. 1768) Presbyterian church. The Colonial nave and the old churchyard are both worth a visit. Old Pine's congregants are very welcoming. ○ *½ hr. (See p 24, 8.)*

10 ★ St. Peter's Episcopal.
When Washington wasn't feasting on potpie and dancing jigs in the Powels' ballroom, he and Martha (1731–1802) were participating in more solemn occasions as members of this circa-1761 house of worship, part of the "breakaway" from England's Anglican church in 1784. ○ *½ hr. (see p 24, 9).*

11 Headhouse Square.
Although this all-brick, open-air market is only a replica of the 1745 original, the site has recently been reborn as a fantastic local farmers' market that's open weekends spring through fall. Flanked by cobblestone streets, the "headhouse" at the top of Pine Street is an 1804 firehouse. ○ *15 min. 2nd St., btw. Pine & Lombard sts.*

12 ★ kids Independence Seaport Museum. Just across Columbus Boulevard, this modern, user-friendly attraction celebrates Society Hill's proximity to the Delaware River (which was, after all, the reason the neighborhood was established). The maritime collection here is first class, but so are the interactive, all-ages exhibits. Especially of note: Workshop on the Water, where visitors can observe classes in traditional wooden boatbuilding and restoration. ○ *1 hr. 211 S. Columbus Blvd. (at Walnut St.)* ☎ *215/413-8655. www.phillyseaport. org. Admission $14 adults, $10 seniors, children, students & military (pay $5 after 5pm in summer to visit just museum OR just ships). Daily 10am–5pm (May 23–Aug open to 7pm on Thurs–Sat).*

City Hall/Midtown

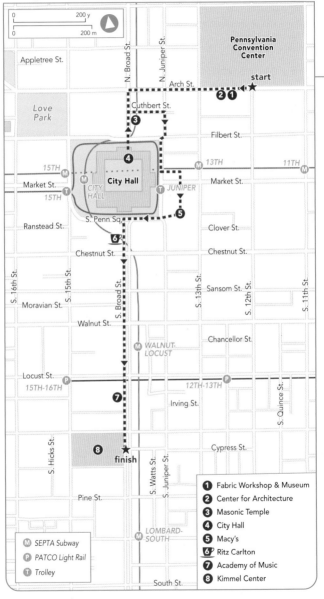

1	Fabric Workshop & Museum
2	Center for Architecture
3	Masonic Temple
4	City Hall
5	Macy's
6	Ritz Carlton
7	Academy of Music
8	Kimmel Center

M SEPTA Subway
P PATCO Light Rail
T Trolley

In the past decade, the heart of Philadelphia has experienced a major renaissance. Broad Street's theaters have grown to become the glittery "Avenue of the Arts;" trendy bistros, shops, and condos transformed a once-dingy corridor of South 13th Street into hip "Midtown Village"; even City Hall has had a facelift and its surrounding Dilworth Plaza turned into a true public space. START: City Hall, Broad & Market sts.

① ★★ Fabric Workshop & Museum. A renovated warehouse—a structure familiar to many Philly artists—houses this unique center for the creation, display, and sale of new work in new materials. Three exhibition galleries and a video lounge show off cutting-edge (and often irresistibly tactile) works of local and international artists. In the permanent collection: Robert Morris' nuclear bed linens, a richly embroidered screen by Carrie Mae Weems, and a rubbery rug by Mona Hatoum. Artists' studios tours are available by appointment, and the gift shop is fantastic. ⏱ *1 hr. 1214 Arch St. (btw. 12th & 13th sts). ☎ 215/561-8888. www.fabricwork shop.org. Admission $3 adults, free for children under 12. Mon–Fri 10am–6pm; Sat–Sun noon–5pm.*

② Center for Architecture. The Philly chapter of the American Institute of Architects offers pristine design exhibits, such as vintage neon and a 3-D model of Center City. The gift-stocked bookstore is worth the trip alone, especially at Christmastime. They also offer $15 city architecture tours Tues, Thurs, and Sat at 2pm (Sat only Dec–Mar). ⏱ *½ hr. 1218 Arch St. ☎ 215/569-3186. www.philadelphiacfa.org. Free admission. Mon–Sat 10am–6pm; Sun noon–5pm.*

③ ★ Masonic Temple. Across from City Hall is a grand lodge of American Freemasonry, a fraternity of obscure, antique origins. A tour of the seven halls offers a crash course in classical architecture— and a glimpse of this fairly secret society where Washington and Franklin were members. ⏱ *1 hr. 1 N. Broad St. ☎ 215/988-1917. www. pagrandlodge.org. Admission $10 adults, $6 students with ID, $5*

The Center for Architecture's bookstore carries fantastic gift items.

The Masonic Temple has ornate classical architecture in seven different halls.

seniors & children 12 & under. Tours Tues–Fri 10am, 11am, 1pm, 2pm, & 3pm; Sat 10am, 11am, & noon.

④ ★★ City Hall. At the center of Center City stands this wedding cake of an all-masonry building, topped off with a 37-foot, 27-ton bronze statue of city "founder" William Penn. Treaty in hand, Penn faces east toward the Delaware River and Penn Treaty Park, where he signed a peace pact with the Native American Leni Lenape (or "Delaware") tribe. City Hall's best

The views are excellent from City Hall's 500-foot-high observation deck.

parts are its exterior sculptures by Alexander Milne Calder (1846–1923) and its glassed-in observation deck, just below Billy Penn, 500 feet above ground with views clear to New Jersey. An overhaul of surrounding Dilworth Plaza, finished in 2013, provides cafe tables, a park for concerts, and a summer fountain/winter ice rink. ⏱ *1 hr. (See p 15, ⑧).*

⑤ Macy's. No worries: You're not here to shop. You're just here to admire the old John Wanamaker's (now a Macy's), one of the nation's oldest department stores. Although a shadow of its former self, this stunning retail arena still alludes to grander days, when proper ladies, before lunching at the store's Crystal Tearoom, met at the bronze eagle statue from the 1904 World's Fair in an seven-story atrium under the world's largest functional pipe organ (28,604 pipes, still frequently played; www.wanamakerorgan. com). Between Thanksgiving and New Year's, the store attracts crowds for its half-hour holiday light show. ⏱ *½ hr. 1300 Market St. (at Juniper St.).* ☎ *215/241-9000. www. macys.com.*

6 ★ **Ritz Carlton.** So, it's a little on the fancy side, but it's worth the couple of extra dollars you'll spend to have coffee and warm soft pretzels amid the marble and beneath the grand dome of this Pantheon-like structure, opened as Girard Bank in 1908—and transformed into a, well, ritzy hotel in 2000. (See p 141.)

7 ★★★ **Academy of Music.** Flickering gas-lit lanterns announce this 19th century opera hall, modeled after Milan's La Scala. Gilded and gorgeous, the Academy is known as the "Grand Old Lady of Locust Street." (Her massive crystal chandelier is to die for.) If possible, catch a performance of the Pennsylvania Ballet, the Opera Company, or even a pop icon like Prince. (See p 129.) 🕐 *15 min.*

8 ★★ **Kimmel Center.** A few blocks south stands Rafael Viñoly's (b. 1944) dramatic glass-and-steel, accordion-shaped performing arts center. Opened in 2001, the Kimmel encompasses a 2,500-seat, cello-shaped orchestra hall; a 650-seat theater for smaller performances; an interactive education center; and soaring,

The eagle and world-famous Wanamaker organ in Macy's atrium.

community-minded Commonwealth Plaza, which often plays host to free performances. Take the elevator to the rooftop garden for a view of Broad Street, also known as the "Avenue of the Arts." (This is the place to get those tickets to the Academy.) Free, 1-hour tours at 1pm daily. 🕐 *½ hr. 300 S. Broad St. (at Spruce St.).* ☎ *215/790-5886. www.kimmelcenter.org. Free admission. Daily 10am–6pm, or 30 min. past last performance.*

The Kimmel Center is home to several performing arts venues.

Rittenhouse

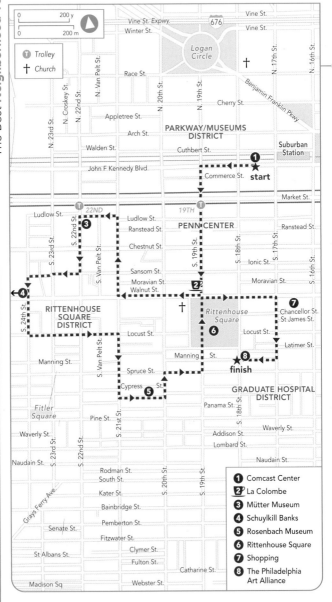

0   200 y
0   200 m

🚋 Trolley
✝ Church

Vine St. Expwy.
Winter St.
Vine St.
Vine St.
676
Logan Circle

Race St.

N. Van Pelt St.
N. 17th St.
N. 16th St.

Benjamin Franklin Pkwy.

Cherry St.

N. 23rd St.
N. Croskey St.
N. 22nd St.
N. 20th St.
N. 19th St.

Appletree St.

Arch St.

PARKWAY/MUSEUMS DISTRICT

Walden St.

Cuthbert St.

Suburban Station

John F Kennedy Blvd.

Commerce St.

❶ ★ **start**

Market St.

Ludlow St.
🚋 22ND
Ludlow St.
🚋 19TH

S. 22nd St.
S. 23rd St.
S. Van Pelt St.
S. 19th St.
S. 18th St.
S. 17th St.
S. 16th St.

❸

Ranstead St.

PENN CENTER

Ranstead St.

Chestnut St.

Sansom St.
Moravian St.
Walnut St.

Ionic St.
Moravian St.

❷

❹

S. 24th St.

RITTENHOUSE SQUARE DISTRICT

✝

Locust St.

Rittenhouse Square

Chancellor St.
St James St.
❼

Locust St.
Latimer St.

❻

Manning St.

Manning St.

❽
★ **finish**

Manning St.
S. Van Pelt St.

Spruce St.

Cypress St.

❺

GRADUATE HOSPITAL DISTRICT

Fitler Square

Pine St.

Panama St.

S. 21st St.
S. 18th St.

Waverly St.

Addison St.
Waverly St.

S. 23rd St.
S. 22nd St.

Naudain St.

Lombard St.

Naudain St.

Rodman St.
South St.

S. 20th St.
S. 19th St.

Kater St.

Bainbridge St.

Grays Ferry Ave.

Pemberton St.

Senate St.

Fitzwater St.

St Albans St.

Clymer St.

Fulton St.

Catharine St.

Madison Sq

Webster St.

❶ Comcast Center
❷ La Colombe
❸ Mütter Museum
❹ Schuylkill Banks
❺ Rosenbach Museum
❻ Rittenhouse Square
❼ Shopping
❽ The Philadelphia Art Alliance

Per capita, more people walk to work in Philadelphia than in any other U.S. city. Many of these pedestrians wind up in this exclusive, residential-meets-commercial neighborhood. If it's a sunny spring day, the Square is the perfect spot to have lunch on a park bench. Fashion tip: If you packed something nice, wear it here. (And if not, take shopping breaks!) START: **19th & Walnut sts.**

① Comcast Center. Philadelphia's tallest building (975 ft.) comes courtesy of the 25 million people who pay Comcast's cable bills. When the Center debuted in 2009, the *Philadelphia Inquirer* called it "a giant USB memory stick." Stop in the atrium to ogle the people "walking" along the overhead beams, and watch a stunning, 83-foot, 10-million-pixel video display above the elevators. A fun aside: In order to break the "curse of William Penn" (that no Philly pro-fessional sports team had won a championship since skyscrapers grew taller than Penn's statue on City Hall), workers attached a figu-rine of Penn to the Center's final beam. A few months later, the Phillies won the World Series. Coincidence? ① *20 min. 1701 JFK Blvd. www.comcast.com. Free admission.*

② **La Colombe.** A Rittenhouse resident wouldn't dream of starting the day without a cappuccino and an almond croissant from this chic cafe. Eat in, and your breakfast will be handed to you on pretty Deruta pottery. *130 S. 9th St.* ☎ *215/563-0860. www.lacolombe.com. $.*

③ ★★ kids Mütter Museum. Visitors—especially kids—will be fascinated, possibly frightened, and definitely grossed out by the huge collection of medical oddities at this dimly lit, 19th-century building that feels straight out of Harry Pot-ter—or, at least, Young Franken-stein. A whopping 20,000 strange-to-creepy objects fill the exhibit spaces at the College of Physicians (no longer a college)—including Grover

The 10-million-pixel video display at the Comcast Center.

The Mütter Museum is filled with medical oddities.

Cleveland's (1837–1908) "secret tumor," a plaster cast of conjoined twins Chang and Eng (1811–1874), John Wilkes Booth's (1838–1865) thorax—and horrifying antique surgical instruments. 🕐 *1½ hr. 19 S. 22nd St. (btw. Market & Chestnut sts.).* ☎ *215/563-3737, ext 293. www.collphyphil.org. Admission $15 adults, $13 seniors & military with ID, $10 students, free 5 & under. Daily 10am–5pm.*

❹ ★ Schuylkill Banks. Another welcome improvement to the cityscape is the extension of the paved riverbank trail from the Art Museum to this neighborhood. Check out what urban progress looks like—and sign yourself up for a kayak lesson while you're here. Entrance at 24th and Locust (cross the tracks) or down the staircase at 24th and Walnut. 🕐 *1 hr. 24th and Locust sts.* ☎ *215/222-6030. www.schuylkillbanks.org.*

❺ ★ Rosenbach Museum. Although it feels like a library, what with the 30,000 rare books and ten times as many precious documents, this grand repository is, in fact, a museum. So, as much as you'd like to leaf through James Joyce's (1882–1941) original Ulysses, peruse a first-edition Melville (1819–1891), or borrow one of Maurice Sendak's (b. 1928) paintings for *Where the Wild Things Are*, you can't—even if the Rosenbach is currently merging with the Free Library. These are artifacts; not loaners. What you may do: Wander about the lovely townhouse into art- and antique-filled rooms left over from the Rosenbachs' time living here. 🕐 *1 hr. 2008–2010 Delancey Place.* ☎ *215/732-1600. www.rosenbach.org. Admission $10 adults, $8 seniors, $5 students, free 4 & under. Tues & Fri noon–5pm, Wed–Thurs noon–8pm, Sat–Sun noon–6pm.*

❻ ★★★ kids Rittenhouse Square. Nearly a century ago, Paul Philippe Cret (1876–1945), designer of Ben Franklin Parkway, gave this park its rather polished good bones. Today, it's the city's most perfect people-watching spot with some charming outdoor sculpture, such as the central plaza's Antoine-Louis Barye's (1796–1875) *Lion Crushing a Serpent* (ca. 1832), Paul Manship's (1885–1966) *Duck Girl*

A paved riverbank trail winds through Schuylkill Banks.

The Rosenbach Museum is home to more than 30,000 rare books.

(ca. 1911) near the reflecting pool, and Albert Laessle's (1877–1954) 2-foot-tall Billy goat in the Square's SW corner—since 1919, the preferred climbing toy of the Square's younger set, who've worn poor Billy's head, horns, and spine to a golden shine. ○ ½ hr. *(See p 46, ❸.)*

❼ ★★ **Shopping.** There's an **Anthropologie** (1801 Walnut St.) inside the Square's Van Rensselaer mansion. Famous scribes sign their latest works at Philly's premier bookseller, **Joseph Fox** (1724 Sansom St.). The display window at **Joan Shepp** (1616 Walnut St.) is downright museum-quality. Even more museum-worthy: the exhibits and shop at **The Print Center** (1514 Latimer St.).

❽ **The Philadelphia Art Alliance.** America's oldest multi-disciplinary art center was opened in 1915 by Christine Wetherill Stevenson in her 1906 family mansion. Its exhibitions range from fashion and artistic textiles to sculpture and prints. You can also grab an excellent meal (though not a cheap one) at the in-house Rittenhouse Tavern, in an elegant dining room or al

fresco on the terrace. ○ ½ hr. 251 S. 18th St. (at Manning St.) ☎ 215/ 545-4302. www.philartalliance.org. Admission $5 adults, $3 students & seniors. Tues–Fri 11am–5pm, Sat–Sun noon–5pm.

Rittenhouse Square contains several pieces of outdoor sculpture.

Fairmount

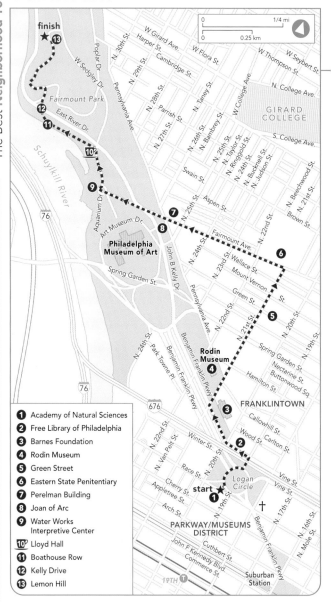

0 — 1/4 mi
0 — 0.25 km

finish ★ 13

W Girard Ave.

Poplar Dr.

W. Sedgley Dr.

Harper St.

Cambridge St.

W Flora St.

W Seybert St.

W Thompson St.

N. College Ave.

GIRARD COLLEGE

S. College Ave.

Fairmount Park

W Taney St.

W College Ave.

N. Bambrey St.

N. Taylor St.

N. Ringgold St.

N. Bucknell St.

N. Judson St.

N. Beechwood St.

N. 21st St.

Brown St.

East River Dr.

Pennsylvania Ave.

Parrish St.

Swain St.

Aspen St.

N. 22nd St.

Schuylkill River

76

Aquarium Dr.

Art Museum Dr.

Philadelphia Museum of Art

John B Kelly Dr.

Spring Garden St.

Fairmount Ave.

Wallace St.

Mount Vernon St.

Green St.

Pennsylvania Ave.

Spring Garden St.

Nectarine St.

Buttonwood Sq.

Hamilton St.

N. 20th St.

N. 19th St.

FRANKLINTOWN

Rodin Museum

Benjamin Franklin Pkwy.

Park Towne Pl.

Callowhill St.

Carlton St.

Wood St.

Winter St.

Race St.

Cherry St.

Appletree St.

Arch St.

PARKWAY/MUSEUMS DISTRICT

John F Kennedy Blvd.

Cuthbert St.

Commerce St.

19TH

Logan Circle

Vine St.

Vine St.

N. 17th St.

N. 16th St.

N. Mole St.

Benjamin Franklin Pkwy.

Suburban Station

start ★

676

① Academy of Natural Sciences
② Free Library of Philadelphia
③ Barnes Foundation
④ Rodin Museum
⑤ Green Street
⑥ Eastern State Penitentiary
⑦ Perelman Building
⑧ Joan of Arc
⑨ Water Works
　 Interpretive Center
⑩ Lloyd Hall
⑪ Boathouse Row
⑫ Kelly Drive
⑬ Lemon Hill

ound by Vine and Girard, Broad and the Schuylkill, Fairmount is often called the "Museum District." And, while it's true that the Philadelphia Museum of Art, Franklin Institute, Barnes Foundation, and Academy of Natural Sciences all exist here, so do some marvelous examples of elegant urban living. START: **19th St. & Ben Franklin Pkwy.**

❶ ★★ kids Academy of Natural Sciences. If it's dinosaurs you seek, look no further. More than a dozen impressive specimens, including a massive T-Rex with jaws agape, are on display in the main hall. On weekends, kids can even "dig" for fossils. This natural history museum is also home to enormous moose, bison, and bears; a second floor filled with Asian and African flora and fauna; a tropical butterfly exhibit; and "Outside in" where kids can touch whatever animals happen to stop by that day. ⏲ *1 hr. 19th St. & Ben Franklin Pkwy.* ☎ *215/299-1000. www.ansp.org. Admission $15 adults, $13 seniors, military, students, & kids 3–12. Mon–Fri 10am–4:30pm, Sat–Sun 10am–5pm.*

❷ Free Library of Philadelphia. Stoic and splendid from its perch at the top of Logan Circle, the central branch of the public library is the best place to delve into writing about local travel and history (second floor). ⏲ *½ hr. 1901 Vine Street.* ☎ *215/686-5322. www. library.phila.gov. Free admission. Mon–Thurs 9am–9pm, Fri 9am–6pm, Sat 9am–5pm, Sun 1–5pm.*

❸ ★★★ Barnes Foundation. Moved here (contentiously) from its original suburban home in 2012, this world-renowned museum is stuffed with some 8,000 largely Impressionist and Post-Impressionist works (Renoir, Cézanne, Matisse, Picassos, Van Gogh) fussily arranged by Barnes himself alongside antique everyday objects (think: iron hinges) and primitive sculpture. ⏲ *2 hrs. 2025 Benjamin Franklin Pkwy.* ☎ *215/278-7000. www.barnesfoundation. org. Reservations highly recommended. Admission $22 adults. Mon, Wed–Thurs 10am–6pm; Fri 10am–10pm; Sat–Sun 10am–8pm.*

❹ ★★ Rodin Museum. It's the largest collection of the master's

The Academy of Natural Sciences boasts a tropical butterfly exhibit among its many attractions.

The Joan of Arc monument was originally commissioned by Napoleon III for Paris.

statues outside Paris. The sculpture garden—including *Thinker* and *Gates of Hell*—is free (see p 15). ⏱ ½ hr.

⑤ Green Street. Stroll this residential thoroughfare to admire beautiful 19th century townhouses. ⏱ *10 min.*

⑥ ★ Eastern State Penitentiary. Smack-dab in the center of Fairmount is this frightening former prison, placed atop the nearest hill to Center City to serve as a warning to criminals. It didn't work: Eastern State stayed in business from 1829 to 1971, and is busiest now around Halloween and Bastille Day (July 14). ⏱ *1 hr. (See p 48, ⑧).*

⑦ ★★ Perelman Building. Across the street from the Philadelphia Museum of Art—which is worth a visit when you have a couple of hours (see p 35, ⑪)—this restored Art Deco office building has textile and design treasures, smaller exhibits, and a lovely cafe. ⏱ *1 hr. (See p 35, ⑫).*

⑧ ★ Joan of Arc. Napoleon III commissioned this gilded equestrian statue of the French heroine in 1874 for Paris. In 1890 the city of Philadelphia asked for a copy, but sculptor Emmanuel Frémiet (1824–1910) gave the original to them instead, sculpting a new version for Paris. (Irony: Valerie Laneau, the 15-year-old model who sat for Joan, died in a fire—though at the ripe old age of 77.) ⏱ *10 min.*

⑨ ★★ kids Water Works Interpretive Center. Behind the Art Museum and atop Fairmount Dam is a charming line of miniature classical facades marking the restored location of the country's first municipal water delivery systems. This center aims to teach the importance of clean water via high-tech exhibits—a simulated helicopter ride takes visitors from the Delaware Bay to the head-waters of the Schuylkill River—and offers an engaging message of environmental awareness.

The Water Works Interpretive Center includes several miniature classical facades.

Kelly Drive is popular with cyclists and joggers.

🕐 *1 hr. 640 Waterworks Dr.* ☎ *215/685-0723. www.fairmount waterworks.com. Free admission. Tues–Sat 10am–5pm, Sun 1–5pm.*

10 **Lloyd Hall.** This newest of boathouses is owned and operated by the City of Philadelphia; despite that, it serves some tasty salads, sandwiches, and pastries. There's also a bike rental stand out front. *1 Boathouse Row (Kelly Dr.).* ☎ *215/978-0900. www.cosmicfoods.com. Mon–Fri 8am–4pm, Sat–Sun 8am–6pm. $.*

11 ★★ **Boathouse Row.** Although these 10 Victorian-era sculling clubhouses are most famously viewed at night from the other side of the river (their lines are trimmed in tiny white lights), they're great to peek into as you pass by. Together they form the "Schuylkill Navy," most often used by college and high school crew teams. Frank Furness (1839–1912) designed no. 13, Undine Barge Club. 🕐 *½ hr. no. 2–14 Boathouse Row, Kelly Dr.*

12 ★★ **Kelly Drive.** Named for champion Olympian oarsman Jack Kelly (father of Grace Kelly [1929–1982]), this winding road has an adjacent path popular with cyclists and joggers (see p 87). Even a short walk here leads to some marvelous sculpture, including one of Kelly himself and, hiding atop a rock, Frederic Remington's (1861–1909) *Cowboy* (ca. 1905). 🕐 *½ hr. Kelly Dr., btw. Fairmount Ave. and Strawberry Mansion Bridge.*

13 ★ **Lemon Hill.** High above Kelly Drive is the summer home of merchant Henry Pratt. Built in the 1800s, this Federal-style "country" estate boasts an impressive trio of stacked oval rooms and serene gardens. 🕐 *½ hr. Sedgeley & Lemon Hill Drive.* ☎ *215/232-4337. www.lemonhill.org. Admission $5 adults, $3 seniors & students. Apr to mid-Dec Thurs–Sun 10am–4pm; Jan–Mar by appt.*

Lemon Hill is a country estate built in 1800.

University City

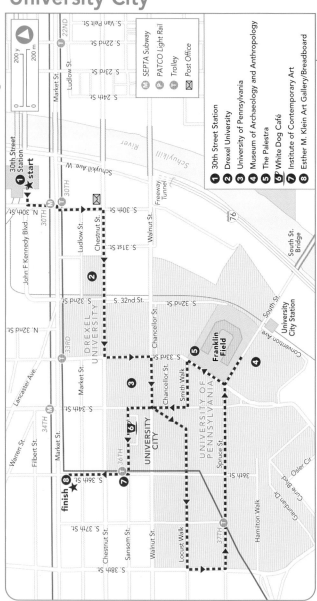

1 30th Street Station
2 Drexel University
3 University of Pennsylvania
4 Museum of Archaeology and Anthropology
5 The Palestra
6 White Dog Café
7 Institute of Contemporary Art
8 Esther M. Klein Art Gallery/Breadboard

M SEPTA Subway
P PATCO Light Rail
T Trolley
X Post Office

West of the Schuylkill River lies Philly's first suburb, known today as University City. Its centerpiece is the University of Pennsylvania, founded in 1740 by (who else but) Franklin and friends, which boasts the country's first medical, law, and business schools. START: **30th St. Station, btw. 29th & 30th sts. on Market St.**

❶ ★★ 30th Street Station.
Twenty thousand Amtrak, SEPTA, and NJ Transit commuters pass daily through this circa-1933 train station, the roof of which was built to accommodate small aircraft landing. Notice the ornate Art Deco decor, the PA Railroad Workers World War II Memorial featuring the Archangel Michael, and the 1895 Spirit of Transportation relief mural in a side chamber. ⏱ *15 min. 2955 Market St.* ☎ *215/580-6500. Daily 24 hr.*

❷ ★★ Drexel University. This high-tech university, founded in 1891, has gone through several name changes, developed a world-class engineering program, and added contemporary architecture, including a dorm by Michael Graves at 33rd and Race sts. ⏱ *1 hr. Btw. 31st & 35th sts, Chestnut & Powelton sts. www.drexel.edu.*

❸ ★★★ University of Pennsylvania. One of the country's oldest universities, "Penn" belongs both to the Ivy League and to the long list of Philadelphia establishments founded by Ben Franklin. The city campus is a mix of modern and antique, with a well-heeled and international student body. Penn's heart is "Locust Walk," a vibrant pedestrian thoroughfare bisecting campus, passing between ivy-covered, 19th-century Gothic buildings; student-populated College Green; giant contemporary sculpture (Claes Oldenburg's [b. 1929] *Split Button*); and modern, Louis Kahn-designed (1901–1974) Fine Arts Library. Look carefully, and find Franklin (in bronze) seated on a park bench, too. ⏱ *½ hr. Woodland Walk to Locust Walk (btw. 34th & 38th sts).* ☎ *215/898-5000. www.upenn.edu.*

❹ ★★★ kids University of Pennsylvania Museum of Archaeology and Anthropology. Since 1887—through 400-some archaeological and anthropological international expeditions—Penn's major museum has collected more than 1 million ancient objects. A vast portion of them are displayed (and intelligently explained) within this massive Beaux Arts building's 25 galleries, distributed among three floors. The Egyptian collection, considered one of the finest in the world, includes a colossal Sphinx, enormous columns, and Mummies, Secrets, and Science, a favorite among families. The third floor's world-renowned excavation display of Sumerian jewelry and household objects from the royal tombs of Ur is not to be missed. Nearby, ogle giant cloisonné lions from Beijing's Imperial Palace, Chinese court treasures, and tomb figures. Basically, if it's ancient, it's here: Mesopotamia; the Bible Lands; Mesoamerica; the ancient Mediterranean; and native

Locust Walk is the heart of the University of Pennsylvania.

The Museum of Archaeology and Anthropology has collected more than 1 million ancient objects.

peoples of the Americas, Africa, and Polynesia are also all represented. Mondays are event days (performances, concerts, special tours); Wednesday mornings often see multicultural kid-friendly performances such as dance, storytelling, drumming, or puppetry. ⏱ *2 hrs. 3260 South St. (a continuation of Spruce St. past 33rd St.).* ☎ *215/898-4000. www.museum.upenn.edu. Admission $15 adults, $13 seniors, $10 students with ID & children 6–17, free 5 & under. Tues–Sun 10am–5pm (to 8pm Wed).*

⑤ ★ The Palestra. If you know college hoops, you know Penn's circa-1927 gymnasium, a.k.a. "The Cathedral of College Basketball." More NCAA men's b-ball games, tournaments, and visiting teams have played here than anywhere else. The tradition continues today, so when you visit, you might catch a St. Joe's, Villanova, Temple, or (of course) Penn game. ⏱ *½ hr. 215 S. 33rd St. (btw. Walnut & Spruce sts.).*

⑥ White Dog Cafe. If you're not lucky enough to pass 34th & Walnut streets weekdays 11am–3pm, when the amazing vegetarian/vegan food truck Magic Carpet is serving (www.magiccarpetfoods.com), continue on to this excellent (if pricey) Philly mainstay of eclectic, organic foods. *3420 Sansom St.* ☎ *215/386-9224. www.whitedog.com. $$.*

⑦ ★★ Institute of Contemporary Art. Edgy modern art is always on display at this spare, Penn-run gallery. The first museum to show Andy Warhol (1928–1987), Laurie Anderson (b. 1947), and Robert Indiana (b. 1928), the ICA's installations have ranged from rocketry to music, and couture to comics. ⏱ *1 hr. 118 S. 36th St. (at Sansom St.).* ☎ *215/898-7108. www.icaphila.org. Free admission. Wed 11am–8pm, Thurs–Fri 11am–6pm, Sat–Sun 11am–5pm.*

⑧ ★ Esther M. Klein Art Gallery/Breadboard. If you have one more stop in you, visit this unique and up-and-coming gallery. EKG puts on contemporary exhibits with a science and technology bent, so that photo you're admiring might have a bio lesson behind it. ⏱ *½ hr. 3600 Market St.* ☎ *215/966-6188. www.breadboardphilly.org/ekg. Free admission. Mon–Sat 9am–5pm.* ●

The Best **Shopping**

Center City **Shopping**

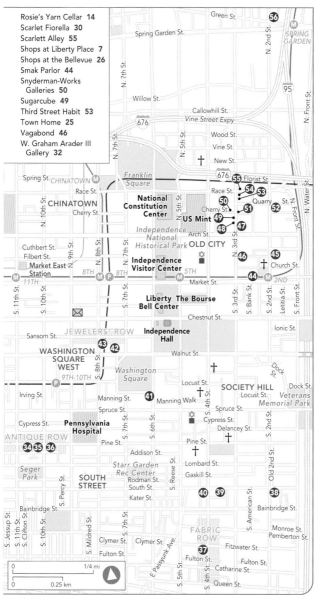

Shopping Best Bets

Best for **Gifts**
★★ Open House, *107 S. 13th St. p 82)*

Best **Bookshop**
★★ Joseph Fox, *1724 Sansom St. (p 82)*

Best for **Precious Baubles**
★★★ Halloween, *1329 Pine St. (p 83)*

Best for **Antiques with Provenance**
★★ M. Finkel & Daughter, *936 Pine St. (p 77)*

Best for **Emerging Art**
★★ Larry Becker Contemporary Art, *43 N. 2nd St. (p 78)*

Best **Children's Shop**
★★ Happily Ever After, *1010 Pine St. (p 79)*

Best **Edible Souvenirs**
★★★ Reading Terminal Market, *12th and Arch sts. (p 83)*

Best for **Crafters**
★★★ Loop, *1914 South St. (p 80)*

Best **Women's Designer Clothing**
★★★ Joan Shepp, *1616 Walnut St. (p 81)*

Best **Edgy Women's Wear**
★★ Vagabond, *37 N. 3rd St. (p 82)*

Best for **Shoes**
★★ Bus Stop Boutique, *727 S. 4th St. (p 84)*

Best for **Browsing**
★ Macy's, *1300 Market St. (p 81)*

Best for **Foodies**
★★ DiBruno Brothers, *1730 Chestnut St. (p 83)*

Best for **Sports Fanatics**
★★ Mitchell & Ness, *1318 Chestnut St. (p 84)*

Best **Cheap and Chic Clothing**
★★ Lost & Found, *133 N. 3rd St. (p 82)*

M. Finkel & Daughter carries antique furnishings and paintings.

Shopping A to Z

Antiques/Vintage

★★ Blendo ANTIQUE ROW
Feels like grandma's attic, with all of the clutter and more of the treasures (including brand-new finds, too). Not the cheapest, though. *1002 Pine St. (btw. 10th & 11th sts.)* ☎ *215/351-9260. www.shopblendo. com. AE, DISC, MC, V. Bus: 23, 40. Map p 74.*

★ Calderwood Gallery NORTH BROAD   Janet and Gary Calderwood's emporium of rare, French Art Deco has expanded into a larger space with 30,000 square feet to showcase 20th century design and photography. *631 N. Broad St. (btw. Mt. Vernon & Wallace sts.)* ☎ *215/546-5357. www.calderwood gallery.com. AE, MC, V. Bus: 4, 16. Subway: Spring Garden. Map p 74.*

★★ Freeman's/Fine Arts of Philadelphia RITTENHOUSE   The local version of Sotheby's or Christy's, with catalogued auctions of art, jewelry, antiques, decorative arts, and fashion. *1808 Chestnut St. (btw. 18th & 19th sts.).* ☎ *215/563-9275. www.freemansauction.com. No credit cards. Bus: 9, 17, 21, 42. Map p 74.*

★★★ Material Culture NORTH-WEST PHILADELPHIA   Worth the ride up to the Nicetown/Queen's Lane area north of Fairmount for a warehouse-sized Aladdin's cave of furnishings, rugs, and home decorations—60,000 square feet of antique, repro, or modern folk Chinese, Turkish, South Asian, American, African, and one-of-a-kind home decorations, often at amazingly low prices. *4700 Wissahickon Ave. (enter on Roberts Ave.; off the Rte. 1 Roosevelt Expwy./Lincoln Hwy.)* ☎ *215/849-8030. www. materialculture.com. AE, MC, V. Bus: H, XH. Map p 74.*

★★ M. Finkel & Daughter ANTIQUE ROW   Known for restored schoolgirl samplers from the 17th through mid-19th century, this well-appointed shop also stocks American folk art, furnishings, and paintings. *936 Pine St. (at 10th St.)* ☎ *215/627-7797. www. samplings.com. AE, MC, V. Bus: 23, 40. Map p 74.*

★★ Mode Moderne OLD CITY   More vintage than antique, the mint-condition furniture at this two-level shop hails from the dawn of the "atomic" modern era; think Charles and Ray Eames, not Chippendale. *159 N. 3rd St. (btw. Arch and Race sts.)* ☎ *215/627-0299. www.modemoderne.com. AE, DISC, MC, V. Bus: 5, 48, 57. Map p 74.*

★★ Moderne Gallery OLD CITY   Robert Aibel's artful collection includes early Nakashima (1905–1990); French ironwork; and sculpture, furnishings, and woodcuts from the American craft movement. *111 N. 3rd St. (btw. Arch & Race sts.).* ☎ *215/923-8536. www. modernegallery.com. MC, V. Bus: 5, 48, 57. Map p 74.*

★★ W. Graham Arader III Gallery CENTER CITY   Rare 16th through 19th-century maps, watercolors, and prints—including some by renowned naturalist John James Audubon (1785–1851)—are the specialty inside Arader's landmark building. *1308 Walnut St.* ☎ *215/ 735-8811. www.aradergalleries.com. AE, MC, V. Bus: 9, 12, 21, 42. Subway: Walnut-Locust. Map p 74.*

Art

★ Eyes Gallery SOUTH STREET   Sometimes religious, often offbeat, and always colorful Latin American folk art bursts from the seams of this multi-floor, 30-something-year-old shop covered in mosaics by local artist Isaiah Zagar. *402 South St. (at 4th St.)* ☎ *215/925-0193. www.eyesgallery.com. AE, DISC, MC, V. Bus: 40, 57. Map p 74.*

★ **Fleisher/Ollman Gallery** RITTENHOUSE   This storied gallery (which moved in 2013 to the same building as the Fabric Workshop; below) carries fine works by emerging contemporary and self-taught American artists. *1216 Arch St. (btw. 12th & 13th sts).* ☎ *215/545-7562. www.fleisher-ollmangallery.com. AE, DISC, MC, V. Bus: 23, 48. Map p 74.*

★★ **Larry Becker Contemporary Art** OLD CITY   An intimate space for new, often spare paintings and sculpture from modern artists such as Marcia Hafif (b. 1929) and John Zinsser (b. 1961). *43 N. 2nd St. (btw. Market & Arch sts.)* ☎ *215/925-5389. Exhibits/info on Facebook. No credit cards. Bus: 17, 21, 33, 42, 48, 57. Subway: 2nd St. Map p 74.*

★★★ **Locks Gallery** WASHINGTON SQUARE   A Beaux-Arts building houses a powerhouse gallery exhibiting big-deal works by de Kooning (1904–1997), Hockney (b. 1937), and Rauschenberg (1925–2008). *600 Washington Sq. (at 6th St., btw. Walnut & Spruce sts.).* ☎ *215/629-1000. www.locksgallery. com. No credit cards. Bus: 9, 12, 21, 42, 47. Map p 74.*

★★ **Minima** OLD CITY   More "design" than "art," the wares in this glossy white space consist of pristinely modern furnishings by Piero Lissoni (b. 1956), Phillippe Starck (b. 1949), Jasper Morrison (b. 1959), and Marcel Wanders (b. 1963). *118 N. 3rd St. (btw. Arch & Race sts.).* ☎ *215/922-2002. www. minima.us. AE, DISC, MC, V. Bus: 5, 48, 57. Map p 74.*

Larry Becker Contemporary Art offers an intimate space for showcasing modern artists.

★ **Newman Galleries** RITTENHOUSE   Philadelphia's oldest gallery (ca. 1865) represents Bucks County artists, American sculptors, and traditional painters. *1625 Walnut St. (btw. 16th & 17th sts.).* ☎ *215/563-1779. www.newman galleries.com. AE, DISC, MC, V. Bus: 2, 9, 12, 21, 42. Map p 74.*

★ **Philadelphia Art Alliance** RITTENHOUSE   A striking mansion on the Square houses three floors of exhibition space for a variety of shows that have included photography, fine craft, and more. *251 S. 18th St. (at Rittenhouse Sq.).* ☎ *215/545-4302. www.philart alliance.org. No credit cards. Bus: 12. Map p 74.*

★ **Snyderman-Works Galleries** OLD CITY   Since the mid 1960s, the conjoined galleries of Rick & Ruth Snyderman have been at the forefront of fine art ceramics, glass, jewelry, fiber, and furniture, exhibiting everyone from Dale Chihuly, Ettore Sottsass, and William Morris to up-and-comers in contemporary studio crafts. *303 Cherry St. (btw. N.*

3rd & N. 4th sts.). ☎ 215/238-9576. www.snyderman-works.com. Bus: 5, 48, 57. Map p 74.

Bookstores

★★ AIA Bookstore/Center for Architecture CENTER CITY Alongside hundreds of books about design and architecture at the American Institute of Architecture's shop are Moleskine journals, modern cards, great office supplies, and holiday decorations. *1218 Arch St. (btw. 12th & 13th sts.).* ☎ *215/ 569-3188. www.aiabookstore.com. AE, DISC, MC, V. Bus: 23, 48. Subway: 13th St. Map p 74.*

★ kids Head House Books SOUTH STREET This neat-as-a-pin neighborhood shop stocks classics, bestsellers, and fantastic children's books—and invites local authors for readings. *619 S. 2nd St. (btw. South & Bainbridge sts.).* ☎ *215/923-9525. www.headhouse books.com. AE, DISC, MC, V. Bus: 40, 57. Map p 74.*

★★ Joseph Fox Bookshop RITTENHOUSE Philly's premier book store. This tiny walkup is cozy and well organized, and has a bookish staff who know their stock inside and out. Co-sponsors the readings/ signings of literary heavyweights at the Free Library and other venues. *1724 Sansom St. (btw. 17th & 18th sts.).* ☎ *215/563-4184. www.fox bookshop.com. AE, MC, V. Bus: 2, 9, 12, 21, 42. Map p 74.*

Children's

★ Born Yesterday RITTENHOUSE For the Bugaboo stroller set, a haute boutique for hand-knit sweaters, French onesies, and trendy ensembles for newborns on up. *1901 Walnut St. (across from Rittenhouse Sq.).* ☎ *215/568-6556. www.bornyesterdayphila.com. AE,*

DISC, MC, V. Bus: 9, 12, 17, 21, 42. Map p 74.

★ Children's Boutique RITTENHOUSE Design-your-own cotton sweaters and kiddie "it" brands, plus shoes, toys, and très impressive baby shower baskets. *1702 Walnut St. (btw. 17th & 18th sts.).* ☎ *215/732-2661. www.echildrens boutique.com. AE, DISC, MC, V. Bus: 2, 9, 12, 21, 42. Map p 74.*

★★ Happily Ever After WASHINGTON WEST Classic wooden and tin toys, collectible dolls, puppets and marionettes, and plenty of toys with vintage mid/late-20th century pop culture themes to reawaken parents' inner children— plus the friendliest sales staff of any kids' store in Philly. *1010 Pine St. (btw. 10th & 11th sts.).* ☎ *215/627-5790. www.happily.com. AE, DISC, MC, V. Bus: 23, 40. Map p 74.*

Lolli Lolli WASHINGTON SQUARE This cheerful walk-up stocks classic toys, cute placemats, and plenty of oh-so-adorable clothes for children through age 12. *713 Walnut St. (across from Washington Sq.).*

Joseph Fox Bookshop has hosted readings from the likes of David Sedaris.

215/625-2655. www.lollilolli.net. AE, DISC, MC, V. Bus: 9, 12, 21, 42, 47. Map p 74.

★ **Scarlet Fiorella** CENTER CITY For hip and trendy parents (and their babes) who dig ironic onesies and vintage rock band tees in size 2T. Bonus: stylish clothing and intriguing jewelry for Mom as well. 113 S. 13th St. (btw. Chestnut & Sansom sts.). 215/922-1955. www. scarletfiorella.com. AE, DISC, MC, V. Bus: 9, 21, 38, 42, 124. Map p 74.

Crafts

★★ **Art Star** NORTHERN LIBERTIES If you like Etsy, you'll love this youthful gallery's stock of handmade clothing, accessible art, and sculptural jewelry. 623 N. 2nd St. (btw. Spring Garden St. & Fairmount Ave.). 215/238-1557. www.art starphilly.com. MC, V. Bus: 5, 25, 43, 57. Subway: Spring Garden St. Map p 74.

★★ **The Clay Studio** OLD CITY This not-for-profit studio founded in the 1970s by a quintet of Philly artists is the serious, art-focused progenitor to those paint-your-own-pot chain stores. Inspired by the artist-produced pottery in the shop? Sign up for a half-day workshop. 137–139 N. 2nd St. (btw. Arch & Race sts.). 215/925-3453. www.theclay studio.org. Bus: 5, 48, 57. Subway: 2nd St. Map p 74.

★★ **The Fabric Workshop and Museum** CENTER CITY Noted artists-in-residence work with skilled printmakers and promising apprentices at this not-for-profit center to produce a range of artistic products and printed objects. Bonus: You can watch the workshop at work, plus the museum stages buzz-worthy exhibitions. 1214 Arch St. (btw. 12th & 13th sts.). 215/561-8888. www.fabricworkshopandmuseum.org. MC, V. Bus: 23, 48. Subway: 11th St. Map p 74.

★★★ **Loop** SOUTH STREET/RITTENHOUSE This colorful, gallery-like, always friendly shop offers beautiful yarns, pretty fabrics, and tons of patterns (and advice). 1914 South St. (btw. 19th & 20th sts.). 215/893-9939. www.loopyarn. com. DISC, MC, V. Bus: 17, 40. Map p 74.

Rosie's Yarn Cellar RITTENHOUSE This below-ground shop has fueled the knitting pastimes of hundreds of Philadelphians. 2017

Classic toys at Happily Every After are a hit with both kids and parents.

Loop has a wide range of colorful patterns for crafts.

Locust St. (btw. 20th & 21st sts.).
☎ *215/977-9276. www.rosiesyarn
cellar.com. AE, DISC, MC, V. Bus: 9,
12, 17, 21, 42. Map p 74.*

Department Stores/Shopping Centers

★ **Macy's** MIDTOWN This
standby stands out for its antique,
30,000-pipe organ (largest opera-
tional one in the world), multi-story
marble atrium, and holiday light
show—carryovers from its days as
John Wanamaker's, one of the
country's first department stores.
*Btw. 13th & Juniper sts., Chestnut &
Market sts.* ☎ *215/241-9000. www.
macys.com. AE, DISC, MC, V. Bus: 4,
16, 17, 27, 31, 32, 33, 44, 48, 62, 124,
125. Subway: City Hall or 13th St.
Map p 74.*

★ **Shops at Liberty Place** RIT-
TENHOUSE This mini mall, on the
first few levels of one of the city's
tallest buildings, has J. Crew,
Express, Jos. A. Bank, LOFT, Aveda,
and about a dozen more stores.
*Btw. 16th & 17th sts., Chestnut &
Market sts.* ☎ *215/851-9055. www.
shopsatliberty.com. Bus: 2, 17, 31,
32, 33, 38, 44, 48, 62, 124, 125 Subway: 15th St. Map p 74.*

Fashion

★ **Boyd's** RITTENHOUSE Selling
bespoke suits, $25,000 watches,
Dolce & Gabbana frocks, and
Manolo Blahniks, this family-run
business occupies a beautiful old
building and has a staff of obses-
sively attentive salespeople and 65
tailors. *1818 Chestnut St. (btw. 18th
& 19th sts.).* ☎ *215/564-9000. www.
boydsphila.com. AE, DISC, MC, V.
Bus: 9, 17, 21, 42. Map p 74.*

★★★ **Joan Shepp** RITTEN-
HOUSE The mother-daughter
doyennes of the local fashion scene

*This Macy's location was one of the first
department stores in the country.*

run this industrial-chic boutique, where big-deal designers (such as Yohji Yamamoto, Stella McCartney, Dries Van Noten, and Pierre Balmain) come to roost. *1616 Walnut St. (btw. 16th & 17th sts.).* ☎ *215/735-2666. www.joanshepp.com. AE, DISC, MC, V. Bus: 2, 9, 12, 21, 42. Map p 74.*

★ **Knit Wit** RITTENHOUSE The go-to boutique for generations of neighborhood fashionistas offers essentials from Miu Miu, Habitual, and Bluemarine, plus estate jewelry. *1729 Chestnut St. (btw. 17th & 18th sts.).* ☎ *215/564-4760. www.knitwit online.com. AE, DISC, MC, V. Bus: 2, 9, 21, 42.*

★★ **Lost & Found** OLD CITY A mother-daughter team runs this new-plus-vintage shop, known for its reasonable prices on cute, youthful clothing for men and women, Orla Kiely bags, and fun jewelry. *133 N. 3rd St. (btw. Arch & Race sts.).* ☎ *215/928-1311. AE, DISC, MC, V. Bus: 5, 48, 57. Map p 74.*

★ **Smak Parlour** OLD CITY Adorable designers Abby Kessler and Katie Lofuts create each trendy skirt, flirty dress, and cool top in this girly shop, which also sells a smattering of shoes, jewelry, and gifts. *219 Market St. (btw. 2nd & 3rd sts.).* ☎ *215/625-4551. www.smakparlour. com. AE, DISC, MC, V. Bus: 5, 17, 33, 48. Subway: 2nd St. Map p 74.*

★★ **Sugarcube** OLD CITY Up-and-coming labels are the not-inexpensive specialty of this mostly women's and men's shop, a must for the fashion set. *124 N. 3rd St. (btw. Arch and Race sts.).* ☎ *215/238-0825. www.sugarcube.us. AE, MC, V. Bus: 5, 48, 57. Map p 74.*

★★ **Third Street Habit** OLD CITY Philly's version of Barney's women's department, with great designers like Dagmar, Hudson, Isabel Marant, and Rag & Bone. *153 N. 3rd St. (btw. Quarry & Race sts.)* ☎ *215/925-5455. www.thirdstreet habit.com. AE, MC, V. Bus: 5, 48, 57. Map p 74.*

★★ **Vagabond** OLD CITY This pioneering women's shop offers Uzi, LHOOQ, Ace & Jig, plus knits and dresses by the shop's stylish owners. *37 N. 3rd St. (btw. Market & Arch sts.).* ☎ *267/671-0737. www. vagabondboutique.com. AE, DISC, MC, V. Bus: 5, 48, 57. Subway: Market-Frankford Line. Map p 74.*

Gifts

★★ **Duross & Langel** CENTER CITY This emporium of made-in-house body care products doesn't have shoppers; it has acolytes. It's a locavore's Lush—only better—with bespoke soaps, fragrances, body washes, shampoos, scented candles, aromatic oils, and more. *117 S. 13th St. (at Sansom St.).* ☎ *215/592-7627. www.durossandlangel.com. AE, DISC, MC, V. Bus: 9, 12, 21, 38, 42, 124. Subway: Walnut-Locust. Map p 74.*

★ **Hello Home/Hello World** ANTIQUE ROW/RITTENHOUSE Restored vintage furnishings, great new shelter pieces, pretty jewelry, and kids' clothes combine in these two neighborhood shops. *Hello Home: 1004 Pine St. (btw. 10th & 11th sts.).* ☎ *215/545-7060. Bus: 23. Hello World: 257 S. 20th St. (btw. Locust & Spruce sts.).* ☎ *215/545-5207. www.shophelloworld.com. AE, DISC, MC, V. Bus: 12,17. Map p 74.*

★★ **Open House** CENTER CITY Bright vases, clever pillows, pretty coffee cups, great kiddie goodies, and wonderful bath products make this one of the best spots for gift shopping—for yourself. *107 S. 13th St. (btw. Sansom & Chestnut sts.).* ☎ *215/922-1415. www.openhouse living.com. Bus: 9, 21, 38, 42, 124. AE, MC, V. Map p 74.*

★★ Scarlett Alley OLD CITY
For fantastic, unexpected, stylish souvenirs like Italian cordial glasses, hand-painted bowls, and great table linens. *241 Race St. (btw. 2nd & 3rd sts.).* ☎ *215/592-7898. www. scarlettalley.com. AE, MC, V. Bus: 5, 57. Map p 74.*

★★ Town Home RITTENHOUSE
Pretty, extra-petite shop known for its amazing jewelry by the likes of Me&Ro, Kasey K., and Heather Moore, plus inimitable Alora diffusers and chic baby onesies.*1616 Walnut St.* ☎ *215/972-5100. www. townhomeonline.com. AE, MC, V. Bus: 2, 9, 12, 21, 42. Map p 74.*

Gourmet Food
★★ DiBruno Brothers RITTEN-
HOUSE Locals think this two-floor shop with its cheese cave and cafeteria is better than Dean & DeLuca. They're right. *Original, Italian Market location: 930 S. 9th St.* ☎ *215/922-2876. Central location: 1730 Chestnut St. (btw. 17th & 18th sts.).* ☎ *215/665-9220. www.dibruno. com. AE, DISC, MC, V. Bus: 9, 17, 21, 42. Map p 74.*

★★★ Reading Terminal Market CENTER CITY This charming,
80-stall indoor market has oysters, organic produce, ice cream, cookbooks, chocolates, sushi, tacos, gourmet cheeses, Pennsylvania Dutch pretzels, roast pork sandwiches, moon pies . . . *12th St. (btw. Arch & Filbert sts.).* ☎ *215/922-2317. www.readingterminalmarket. org. Some kiosks accept some credit cards. Bus: 23, 48, 61. Subway: 13th St. Map p 74.*

Jewelry
★★★ Halloween ANTIQUE
ROW With only an orange business card in the window as signage, this boutique feels like a treasure trove with pearls upon pearls, opals upon opals, silver upon silver— including vintage and custom pieces. *1329 Pine St. (at Juniper St.).* ☎ *215/732-7711. No credit cards. Bus: 4, 27, 32, 40. Subway: Lombard South. Map p 74.*

Jeweler's Row WASHINGTON
SQUARE A couple blocks' worth of wholesale and retail merchants around Samson Street, whose vibe ranges from pawn shop to antiques shop. Jeweler's Row is tailored to sellers of gold and buyers of engagement rings. *Btw. 7th & 8th sts., Walnut & Chestnut sts. Bus: 9, 21, 42, 47. Subway: 8th St. Map p 74.*

★ Lagos RITTENHOUSE Flag-
ship for a local jeweler who made the big time (his line is now carried in all the chic department stores),

Cheese plays a starring role at the multi-level DiBruno Brothers.

known for its fashion-forward settings, colored gems, and beaded look. Oprah is a fan. *1735 Walnut St. (btw. 17th & 18th sts.).* ☎ *215/567-0770. www.lagos.com. AE, MC, V. Bus: 9, 12, 21, 42. Map p 74.*

Shoes

★ Benjamin Lovell Shoes

SOUTH STREET/RITTENHOUSE Locally based chain best known for its comfort footwear from Merrell, Ugg, Ecco, Dansko, and Naot, plus fresh kicks from Camper and Cole Haan. *South St.: 318 South St. (btw. 3rd & 4th sts.).* ☎ *215/238-1969. Bus: 40, 57. Rittenhouse: 119 S. 18th St. (btw. Sansom & Chestnut sts.).* ☎ *215/564-4655. Bus: 9, 12, 21, 42. www.benjaminlovellshoes.com. AE, DISC, MC, V. Map p 74.*

★★ Bus Stop Boutique QUEEN

VILLAGE Super-friendly British shopkeep Elena Brennan maintains a stylishly offbeat selection of women's and men's shoes, bags, and jewelry from cutting-edge European and local designers. *727 S. 4th St. (btw. Fitzwater & Catharine sts.).* ☎ *215/627-2357. www.busstop boutique.com. AE, DISC, MC, V. Bus: 57. Map p 74.*

Sporting Goods

★★ Mitchell & Ness Sporting

Goods CENTER CITY Find authentic, licensed replicas of the jerseys, caps, and jackets of some

Halloween features vintage and custom jewelry pieces.

The fashion choices at Bus Stop Boutique are stylishly offbeat.

of America's best-known athletes. *1201 Chestnut St. (btw. 12th & 13th sts.).* ☎ *866/879-6485. www.mitchell andness.com. AE, DISC, MC, V. Bus: 9, 21, 23, 38, 42. Subway: Walnut-Locust or 13th St. Map p 74.*

★ The Original I. Goldberg

CENTER CITY This classic army-navy outfitter sells everything you need to spend the night outdoors, cheap. Camping gear bought here at age 11 saw me all the way through Eagle Scout. *1300 Chestnut St. (at 13th St.).* ☎ *215/925-9393. igoco.com. AE, DISC, MC, V. Bus: 9, 21, 38, 42, 124. Subway: Walnut-Locust or 13th St. Map p 74.*

★ Philadelphia Runner RITTEN-

HOUSE More than 250 styles of running and walking shoes are for sale at the retail home of the Philadelphia Running Club. *1601 Sansom St. (at 16th St.).* ☎ *215/972-8333. www.philadelphiarunner.com. AE, DISC, MC, V. Bus: 2, 9, 12, 21, 42. Map p 74.*

★★ Rittenhouse Sports Spe-

cialties RITTENHOUSE Forgot your sneaks? Come here, and foot expert Karen McGovern won't just find you a replacement; she'll find you an improvement. *1717 Chestnut St. (btw. 17th & 18th sts.).* ☎ *215/ 569-9957. www.rittenhousesports. com. AE, DISC, MC, V. Bus: 2, 9, 21, 42. Map p 74.* ●

Fairmount Park by Bike

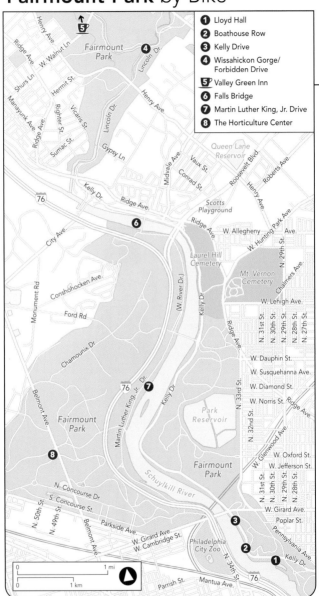

1. Lloyd Hall
2. Boathouse Row
3. Kelly Drive
4. Wissahickon Gorge/ Forbidden Drive
5. Valley Green Inn
6. Falls Bridge
7. Martin Luther King, Jr. Drive
8. The Horticulture Center

Previous page: A cyclist enjoys Philadelphia's abundant green space.

More than 215 miles of trails exist within the 9,200-plus acres that make Fairmount Park the world's largest landscaped city park (for comparison: NYC's Central Park is a mere 843 acres). This 18 to 22-mile route explores areas easiest accessed from Center City, via trails that are paved or gravel-covered, beginner-friendly, and bucolic. START: Lloyd Hall, 1 Boathouse Row, behind the Philadelphia Museum of Art.

1 Lloyd Hall. This community boathouse has a bike-rental shack operated by Wheel Fun Rentals that's open whenever it's sunny and over 55°F. ① ¼ hr. *1 Boathouse Row.* ☎ *215/232-7778. www.wheel funrentals.com. Rentals from $10/hr.; $32/day. 9am–sunset (10am Sept–Oct and on weekdays in Apr and May). Nov–Mar weekends only, 10am–sunset (see "Bike Rentals" on p 161 for other options, including winter weekdays).*

2 ★★ Boathouse Row. You'll quickly whiz by these 10 Victorian-era crew-team clubhouses, so take some time to peep inside; note no. 13, Undine Barge Club, designed by Frank Furness (1839–1912); and perhaps see a college or high school athlete preparing to go sculling. ① *10 min.*

3 ★★ Kelly Drive. For about 4 miles, you'll ride between the Schuylkill (pronounced "Skoo-kill") River and this winding road peppered with sculptures and named after champion oarsman John B. "Jack" Kelly Sr. (1899–1960), winner of three Olympic gold medals and father to Princess Grace Kelly (and to John, Jr., himself a 4-time Olympian). The Drive ends in a sharp left at Ridge Avenue, just after crossing Wissahickon Creek. The trail continues (after a harrowing mile down busy Main Street through trendy Manayunk) all the way to Valley Forge and beyond, but we're going to cross Ridge here at the light and pick up a spur trail, the Wissahickon Bike Trail. ① *45 min.*

4 ★★★ Wissahickon Gorge/ Forbidden Drive. After following

The 1,800-acre Wissahickon Gorge is one of the city's jewels.

The Best of the Outdoors

the trail along Lincoln Drive for 1.3 miles, you will come to a small parking lot where you can turn left onto Forbidden Drive—a 1920s nickname, from when cars were banned, that stuck. This is the jewel of the park system, 1,800 acres of urban nature. The wide, gravelly, wooded trail rises and falls for 5.3 miles. Rocks rise on your left, the wide Wissahickon (Lenape Indian for "catfish creek") flows below to the right. Stop to spot owls, titmice, woodpeckers (5 species nest here), bluebirds, cardinals, nuthatches, goldfinches, and plenty of mallards. Note the 19th-century stone bridges and the Thomas Mill Road covered bridge (built in 1737)—not to mention the many 1930s-era WPA-built shelters. There's no wading in the creek, and a permit is required to explore dirt trails by bike (both widely ignored ordinances). Cellphone service is spotty. ⏱ *2 hrs. Fairmount Park:* ☎ *215/683-0200; www.fairmountpark.org. The Friends of the Wissahickon (a good resource for park news and information):* ☎ *215/247-0417; www.fow.org.*

5 ★ **Valley Green Inn.** This charming, circa-1850 former roadhouse tavern (the last one left in the park) serves sit-down meals—chicken salad sandwiches, salmon clubs, and spinach salads—and has a walk-up stand for drinks and snacks. *Valley Green Rd. at Wissahickon.* ☎ *215/247-1730. www.valleygreeninn.com. $$.*

6 **Falls Bridge.** Turn around to return the way you came—except once back on Kelly Drive, cross the river on this steel Pratt truss bridge built in 1894–95, a low tunnel of lacy steel struts, to head to Martin

The Valley Green Inn is a perfect place to stop and refuel.

Luther King, Jr. Drive. (From the far end of Valley Green, about 7.3 miles.) ⏱ *1 hr.*

7 ★ **Martin Luther King, Jr. Drive.** Weekend days in April through October, this tree-lined thoroughfare (which you'll usually hear referred to as simply "West River Drive") is closed to vehicular traffic. Spread out, enjoy the smooth ride. (There's also a parallel bike trail for when the road's open to traffic, but frost heaves leave it eternally bumpy.) If you're worn out, continue on all the way back, passing the Philadelphia Zoo on your right (see p 45, bullet **9**), crossing back over the river and in front of the Philadelphia Museum of Art (see p 13, bullet **2**) then behind it past the Water Works (see p 68, bullet **9**), and back to Lloyd Hall. (Total from Falls Bridge: 5 miles.) If you're up for more scenery, take a right after 2.1 miles at the trail next to Montgomery Drive (just past the

Fairmount Park by Other Means

By sneaker or skate: If the sun's out, so are the runners, walkers, and bladers along Kelly and MLK Jr. drives. From the Philadelphia Museum of Art, over Strawberry Mansion Bridge (at Ford Rd.) and back is 6.5 miles (10.4 km); go as far as the Falls Bridge (at Calumet St.), and you'll cover 8.5 miles (13.7km). Beware bikers—and resident Canada geese. **By kayak:** Get a river tour by kayak (including lesson, if needed) from the **Hidden River Outfitters,** 25th and Walnut sts. (entrance at 25th and Locust sts.; ☎ 215/222-6030, ext 103; www.hiddenriveroutfitters.com; tours $40–$75; various hours Sat–Sun Jun–Oct), at Schuylkill Banks (www.schuylkillbanks.org)—or, for more advanced paddlers, a day trip to Bartram's Garden.

Columbia Railroad Bridge) for an uphill 0.6 miles, and turn left at Belmont Mansion Drive to the next stop. ① ½ hr.

⑧ ★★★ The Horticulture Center. In order to enjoy this park-within-a-park, you really must dismount. By foot, you can explore all 27 acres of elegant statuary, ponds, pools, tropical plants, fountains, gazebos, and butterflies. A must-visit while you're here: **Shofuso,** a Japanese garden and teahouse (☎ 215/878-5097; www.shofuso.com; May–Sept Wed–Fri 10am–4pm, Sat–Sun 11am–5pm; Apr & Oct Sat–Sun 11am–5pm; admission $6 adults, $4 seniors and students). Renowned architect Yoshimura Junzo (1908–1997) designed the Japanese house in 1953 in Nagoya. Five years later, it landed here, surrounded by lush moss, weeping cherry trees, and koi ponds. Inside are contemporary murals by Hiroshi Senju (b. 1958) and, occasionally, formal tea ceremonies. ① 2 hrs. Belmont Ave. & Montgomery Dr. ☎ 215/685-0048 or 215/685-0096.

www.fairmountpark.org. Free admission. Daily Nov–Mar 8am–5pm, Apr–Oct 8am–6pm.

When you're through here, retrace your tracks back to MLK, Jr. Drive, where you'll take a right toward Center City and head back to Lloyd Hall, about 3½ miles.

The Shofusu Japanese garden is full of elegant ponds and fountains.

Park It: **Five Squares**

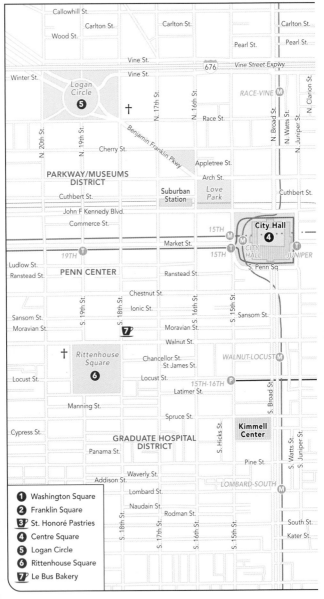

1 Washington Square
2 Franklin Square
3 St. Honoré Pastries
4 Centre Square
5 Logan Circle
6 Rittenhouse Square
7 Le Bus Bakery

The Best of the Outdoors

I n 1682, William Penn planned five green squares for his "Green Countrie Towne." Because of his modest Quaker values, he named the spaces after their locations (Northwest Square, Centre Square), not proper names. Today, Penn's parks are named and, somewhat ironically, are also the city's proudest al fresco showpieces. You can easily see them all in 1 day. START: **6th & Locust sts.**

❶ ★★ Washington Square.

The most historically significant park on the list, the 6½-acre "Southeast Square" was once pasture with a pair of fishable creeks. Starting in 1704, a portion of these grounds became a modest burial ground for the city's unknown and poor, a potter's field. In 1776, troops who died fighting in the burgeoning Revolutionary War were interred here, as were victims of yellow fever in 1793. At the park's center, an eternal flame and bronze statue of Washington serve as the Tomb of the Unknown Revolutionary Soldier. In later years, Washington Square became the centerpiece of the city's active publishing business, with the still-extant *Farm Journal* (in the southwest corner) and **Curtis Publishing Company** (occupying all of Walnut St. between 6th and 7th sts.), once the home of *Ladies' Home Journal* and the *Saturday Evening Post*. Stop in the Curtis Building (through the 7th St. entrance) and walk toward 6th Street to see Maxfield Parrish (1870–1966) and Louis Comfort Tiffany's (1848–1933) gorgeous, 100,000-mosaic **Dream Garden mural,** a hidden gem. Also available for your perusal (on weekdays) is the **Athenaeum** (219 S. 6th St.; ☎ 215/925-2688), an elegant collections library of rare books. ⏱ *1 hr. Btw. 6th & 7th, Spruce & Walnut sts.*

❷ ★★★ kids Franklin Square.

The most recently refreshed of the squares is the most kid-friendly, too. In 2006, after years of neglect, the city cleaned up the space and added 18 holes of Philadelphia-themed

Franklin Square is one of the most kid-friendly spaces in the city.

mini-golf, toddler-to-tween-friendly jungle gyms, a giant sand sculpture, a large and lovely carousel, benches for "Once Upon A Nation" performers, and the really fantastic Square Shack for better-than-average burgers, shakes, and fries. The best time to visit is in spring through fall, when the amusements are up and running. ⏱ *1 hr. (See p 38, bullet ❸.)*

❸ ★★ St. Honoré Pastries. On

your way between the squares, you'll hit Chinatown, where you'll find this bakery and its just-baked Hong Kong buns stamped with lucky red characters and stuffed with sweet sesame, red bean, or azuki fillings. Other specialties of this walk-up shop include mango shakes, tiny cakes, and pastry-wrapped hot dogs. *935 Race St.* ☎ *215/925-5298. $.*

④ Centre Square. This least green (more granite-hued) of squares was once on the outskirts of the city. Today, it's the gray home of ornate City Hall (see p 15, bullet **⑧**), offering only a few trees on its western side, a plot formally known as Dilworth Plaza, named after beloved 1950s mayor Richardson Dilworth (1916–1997). ⏱ *15 min. Broad & Market sts.*

⑤ ★★ Logan Circle. The only square that became a circle, "Northwest" is the nearly bucolic jewel of Ben Franklin Parkway, a boulevard that 20th-century architect Paul Philippe Cret (1876–1945) modeled after the Champs-Elysées to connect City Hall with the Art Museum. Logan's centerpiece is Alexander Stirling Calder's (1870–1945) Swann Fountain (see p 33, bullet **⑦**), with its sky-high arcs of water and three giant bronze horses surrounded by turtles, nymphs, and angels. The square is surrounded by many cultural landmarks: the central branch of the **Free Library of Philadelphia** (see p 67, bullet **②**), the **Franklin Institute** (see p 47, bullet **⑤**), the **Academy of Natural Sciences** (see p 67, bullet **①**), and the 1846

Cathedral Basilica of St. Peter and Paul (pop in for the refreshing cool darkness, and to peek at the dome's frescoes by Constantino Brumidi, famous for his paintings in the Capitol Building in D.C.; ☎ 215/561-1313; www.cathedralphila.org). ⏱ *½ hr. 19th & Race sts.*

⑥ ★★ kids Rittenhouse Square. "Southwest Square" is the best known and highest (foot) trafficked of the group. This sublime urban landscape, with its tall sycamores, diagonal paths, reflecting pool, and scattered sculpture is also the work of Cret (see above). If you plan to sit on a bench and people-watch at anyplace on this list, do it here, paying special attention to the comings and goings around the Rittenhouse Hotel (see p 141), which seems to be the preferred overnight spot for movie stars in town for filming. Rittenhouse is even pretty on winter evenings, when its trees glitter with giant ornament lights. ⏱ *1 hr. Btw. 18th & 19th sts., Walnut & Rittenhouse sts.*

⑦ ★ Le Bus Bakery. Grab a cold drink, a just-grilled panini (try the tuna or roast beef), a chocolate-chip cookie to go, and a bench in the Square, and you're all set. *135 S. 18th St. (btw. Walnut & Sansom sts.).* ☎ *215/569-8299. lebusbakery. com. $.*

Rittenhouse Square is a prime spot to relax and indulge in some people-watching.

Penn's Landing

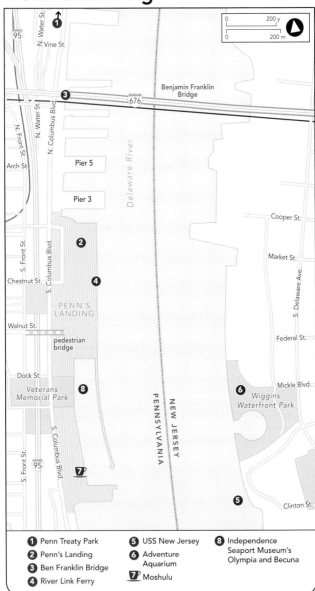

1 Penn Treaty Park
2 Penn's Landing
3 Ben Franklin Bridge
4 River Link Ferry
5 USS New Jersey
6 Adventure Aquarium
7 Moshulu
8 Independence Seaport Museum's Olympia and Becuna

Spanned by Ben Franklin Bridge and bordered by tree and ship-lined shores, the wide Delaware River has been the subject of much recent controversy regarding dredging and gambling (as for the latter: Philly is now the no. 2 gaming market in America, behind Vegas). For now, the riverfront retains a few nice stretches to explore, and even hop a ferry to Camden. START: **Penn Treaty Park.**

① Penn Treaty Park. Formerly Shackamaxon, a village of the Native American Leni Lenape tribe, this riverside park hosted the 1683 meeting of William Penn and chief Tamanend, who stood under an elm to sign a peace treaty that endured 99 years. Today, the tranquil, loosely landscaped plot is bordered by industry and features a small obelisk where the elm once stood. Walk 3 blocks south, past SugarHouse Casino, to Frankford Avenue to catch the 25 bus down Delaware Avenue to Penn's Landing. ○ ½ hr. *Columbus Blvd & Beach St. (off of Delaware Ave.).*

② ★ Penn's Landing. Philadelphia started out as a major freshwater port, and as recently as 1945, 155 "finger" piers jutted out into the river. Today, 14 remain. Replacing some of them are the more visitor-centric circa-1976 Great Plaza, stretching from Spring Garden Street southward and consisting of a multi-tiered, tree-lined amphitheater, space for summer festivals and concerts, and a fantastic outdoor ice skating "River Rink" in the winter. South of Market Street, there's an esplanade with blue guardrails and charts that identify the New Jersey shoreline opposite. ○ ½ hr. *Columbus Blvd btw. Spring Garden & South sts., Visitor's Center at 301 S. Columbus Blvd.* ☎ *215/629-3200. www.delawareriverwaterfrontcorp. com.*

③ ★ Ben Franklin Bridge. Great cities have great bridges, and this circa-1926 suspension model is Philadelphia's. Paul Cret, architect of the Ben Franklin Parkway and Rittenhouse Square, designed it. At night, each of its cables is lit and its span changes color. Pedestrians and cyclists can make the long climb across (it takes about an hour round-trip), but there's not much to do on the immediate other side (Camden, NJ) other than turn around and come back. ○ *15 min. Entrance at 5th & Vine sts.* ☎ *856/ 968-2255. www.drpa.org. Daily 6am–dusk.*

④ ★★ kids River Link Ferry. Next to the Seaport Museum, catch a ride across the Delaware to Camden, NJ's, riverfront. The scenic trip takes about 10 minutes and deposits you near a pair of attractions (below). ○ *15 min.* ☎ *215/925- 5465. www.riverlinkferry.org. Mon– Thurs 9:30am–6pm, Fri–Sun 9:30am–7pm. Round-trip $7 adults, $6 seniors & children 3–12, free for children under 3.*

⑤ ★ kids USS New Jersey. This giant, circa-1942 battleship,

"River Rink," at the Great Plaza in Penn's Landing, is fantastic for outdoor ice-skating during the winter.

referred to as BB62, is the most decorated of its Iowa-class of "fast battleships." A tour involves climbing ladders, peering into 16-inch gun turrets, cramming into living quarters, and learning a history that stretches from tours in World War II to the Persian Gulf. ⏱ *2 hr. 100 Clinton St., Camden, NJ.* ☎ *866/ 77-6262. www.battleshipnewjersey. org. Admission $22 adults; $17 seniors, veterans & children 5–11; free for children 4 and under, active military, WWII & BB62 vets. Nov–Dec & Feb–Mar Sat–Sun 9:30am–3pm; Apr daily 9:30am–3pm; May–Sept 3 daily 9:30am–5pm; Sept 4–Oct daily 9:30am–3pm. Closed Jan.*

⑥ ★ kids Adventure Aquarium. Two million gallons of water fill this expansive museum of the life aquatic, where hippos bob for heads of lettuce; penguins perform and seals cavort at outdoor arenas; stingrays skim through open tanks; jellyfish morph before your eyes; and, for the right (stratospheric) price, you can feed sea turtles, party with penguins, or swim with

Adventure Aquarium lets you get up close to a wide array of aquatic creatures.

the sharks. Among the must-see animals: alligators in the wild West Africa River Experience, rarely exhibited bluefin tuna in the 760,000-gallon Ocean Realm tank, and small sharks swimming in a petting tank for kids. ⏱ *2 hr. 1 Aquarium Dr., Camden, NJ.* ☎ *856/ 365-3300. www.adventureaquarium. com. Admission $25 adults, $18 children 2–12. Daily 10am–5pm.*

⑦ Moshulu. You'll notice there are few places to grab much more than a hotdog along the waterfront, so head to the top deck of this four-masted ship for a burger and a piña colada. *401 S. Columbus Blvd. (btw. Pine & South sts.).* ☎ *215/923-2500. www.moshulu.com. $$.*

⑧ ★ kids Independence Seaport Museum's *Olympia* **and** *Becuna.* Just south of the Independence Seaport Museum's main building (see p 57, bullet ⑫), this pair of historic ships offers a self-guided glimpse of the U.S. Navy of yore. The larger of the two is the *Olympia*, Admiral Dewey's circa-1892 steel flagship during the Spanish-American War, featuring a restored bridge and handsome, originally furnished examples of an officers' saloon and wardroom, flag officer's cabin, and junior officers' mess. *Becuna* is the 1944-launched submarine that served from World War II into the Cold War, and will impart a newfound appreciation for tight quarters. ⏱ *1 hr.* ●

The Best Dining

Dining Best Bets

Best **Cheesesteak**
★ Cosmi's Deli, *1501 S. 8th St.* (p 104)

Best for **Tapas**
★★★ Amada, *217-219 Chestnut St.* (p 102)

Best for **Variety**
★★★ Reading Terminal Market, *51 N. 12th St.* (p 109)

Best **Steakhouse**
★★ Butcher & Singer, *1500 Walnut St.* (p 103)

Best for **Breakfast**
★ Sam's Morning Glory Diner, *735 S. 10th St.* (p 110)

Best for **Sunday Brunch**
★★★ Fountain Restaurant, *1 Logan Square* (p 106)

Best **Deli**
★ Famous Fourth Street Delicatessen, *700 S. 4th St.* (p 105)

Best for **Burgers**
★★★ Village Whiskey, *114 S. 20th St.* (p 111)

Best **Date Spot**
★★★ Fork, *306 Market St.* (p 105)

Best for **Vegetarians**
★ HipCityVeg, *127 S. 18th St.* (p 106)

Best for **Seafood**
★★ Sansom Street Oyster House, *1516 Sansom St.* (p 108)

Best for **Sushi**
★ Zento, *138 Chestnut St.* (p 112)

Best for **Haute Japanese**
★★ Morimoto, *723 Chestnut St.* (p 108)

Best for **Chinese**
★ Lee How Fook, *219 N. 11th St.* (p 107)

Best for **Gourmet Italian**
★★★ Osteria, *640 N. Broad St.* (p 108)

Best for **Italian-American**
★ Villa di Roma, *936 S. 9th St.* (p 111)

Best for **Israeli Fare**
★★★ Zahav, *237 St. James Pl.* (p 112)

Best for **Pizza**
★ Marra's, *1734 E. Passyunk Ave.* (p 107)

Fork is a great place to take a date. Previous page: The Famous Fourth Street Delicatessen makes some of the city's best sandwiches.

South Philly Dining

Bibou **8**	Pat's King of Steaks **1**
Cosmi's Deli **13**	Ralph's Italian Restaurant **4**
Dimitri's **9**	Sabrina's **5**
Geno's **2**	Sam's Morning Glory Diner **3**
Marra's **11**	Tony Luke's Roast Pork **14**
The Mildred **6**	Victor Café **10**
Paradiso **12**	Villa di Roma **7**

Center City Dining

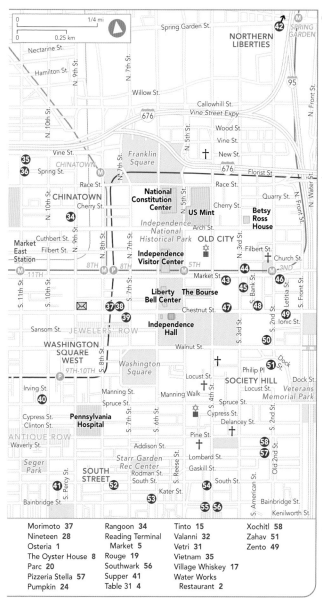

Morimoto **37**
Nineteen **28**
Osteria **1**
The Oyster House **8**
Parc **20**
Pizzeria Stella **57**
Pumpkin **24**

Rangoon **34**
Reading Terminal
    Market **5**
Rouge **19**
Southwark **56**
Supper **41**
Table 31 **4**

Tinto **15**
Valanni **32**
Vetri **31**
Vietnam **35**
Village Whiskey **17**
Water Works
    Restaurant **2**

Xochitl **58**
Zahav **51**
Zento **49**

Dining A to Z

★ **Alma de Cuba** RITTENHOUSE *MODERN CUBAN* Nuevo Latino cuisine—lobster ceviche, Kobe beef tacos, sugarcane tuna—in a Rockwell-designed decor makes for a glamorous night on the town. *1623 Walnut St.* ☎ *215/988-1799. www. almadecubarestaurant.com. Entrees $15–$36. AE, DC, DISC, MC, V. Dinner daily. Bus: 2, 9, 12, 21, 42. Subway: Walnut-Locust. Map p 100.*

★★★ **Amada** OLD CITY *CONTEMPORARY TAPAS* Chic and rustic; don't miss the Spanish cheeses and meats, plantain empanadas, sangria, and flamenco dancing. *217–219 Chestnut St.* ☎ *215/625-2450. www.amadarestaurant. com. Plates $5–$32. AE, DC, DISC, MC, V. Lunch & dinner daily. Bus: 21, 42, 57. Map p 100.*

★ **Audrey Claire** RITTENHOUSE *MEDITERRANEAN BYOB* Grilled Romaine salad, Gorgonzola-and-pear-topped flatbread, and pomegranate roast chicken are on the menu of this stylish little village bistro. *276 S. 20th St. (at Spruce St.).* ☎ *215/731-1222. www.audreyclaire. com. Entrees $17–$27. No credit cards. Dinner daily. Bus: 17. Map p 100.*

★★ **Barclay Prime** RITTENHOUSE *STEAKS* Red meat with a boutique vibe, this low-lit emporium offers Gauchot & Gauchot beef, Kobe sliders, and a splurge-worthy $100 "cheesesteak." *237 S. 18th St. (btw. Locust & Spruce sts.).* ☎ *215/732-7560. www.barclay prime.com. Entrees $30–$75. AE, DC, MC, V. Dinner daily. Bus: 12. Map p 100.*

★ **Beau Monde** SOUTH STREET *FRENCH* Known for its crepes, this pretty, bustling Bretagne-inspired brasserie also serves up lovely salads and romantic ambiance. *624 S. 6th St. (at Bainbridge St.).* ☎ *215/ 592-0656. www.creperie-beaumonde. com. Entrees $4–$22. AE, DC, DISC, MC, V. Lunch & dinner Tues–Sun. Bus: 40, 47. Map p 100.*

★★ **Bibou** BELLA VISTA *FRENCH BYOB* Chanterelles, foie gras, escargots, and very little elbow room: a gem of a bring-your-own-Bordeaux bistro, just off the Italian Market. *1009 S. 8th St. (before Washington Ave.).* ☎ *215/965-8290.*

Rustic Amada has excellent Spanish cuisine.

www.biboubyob.com. Entrees $28–$31. No credit cards. Dinner Tues–Sat. Bus: 47, 47m. Map p 99.

★★ **Bistro 7** OLD CITY *MODERN FRENCH BYOB* A local favorite for green vegetable gazpacho, goat ricotta gnudi, roast chicken, and Peking duck. 7 N. 3rd St. (btw. Market & Arch sts.). ☎ 215/931-1560. www.bistro7restaurant.com. Entrees $28–$32. AE, DC, MC, V. Dinner Tues–Sun. Bus: 17, 33, 48, 57. Subway: 2nd St. Map p 100.

★ **The Blind Pig** NORTHERN LIBERTIES *MODERN AMERICAN* Unpretentious gastro-pub famed for poutine (fries swimming in cheese curds and gravy), blue balls (breaded fried balls of beef, gorgonzola, and mashed potatoes), and dozens of canned beer options. 702 N. 2nd St. (at Fairmount Ave.). ☎ 215/639-4565. www.blindpigphilly.com. Entrees $10–$17. AE, MC, V. Dinner daily; brunch Sun. Bus, 5, 25, 43. Subway: Spring Garden St. Map p 100.

★ **Brauhaus Schmitz** SOUTH STREET *GERMAN* Schnitzel, wieners, brats, spätzle, strudel, and 122 kinds of hearty Belgian and German brews make this convivial *bierhalle* the best wurst place in town. 718 South St. (btw. 7th & 8th sts.). ☎ 267/909-8814. www.brauhausschmitz.com. Entrees $14–$22. Lunch & dinner daily. AE, DC, DISC, MC, V. Bus 40, 47. Map p 100.

★ **Buddakan** OLD CITY *ASIAN FUSION* A trendy spot for lobster fried rice, edamame ravioli, five-spice duck breast, and chocolate pagodas at a communal table beneath a giant gold Buddha. 325 Chestnut St. (btw. 3rd & 4th sts.) ☎ 215/574-9440. www.buddakan.com. Entrees $11–$48. AE, DC, MC, V. Lunch Mon–Fri; dinner daily. Bus: 21, 42, 57. Subway: 2nd St. Map p 100.

★★ **Butcher & Singer** RITTENHOUSE *STEAKS* Beneath the soaring ceiling of an old bank are enormous versions of haute meat-and-potatoes for enormous expense accounts. 1500 Walnut St. (at 15th St.) ☎ 215/732-4444. www.butcherandsinger.com. Entrees $27–$48. AE, DC, MC, V. Lunch Mon–Fri; dinner daily. Bus: 9, 12, 21, 42. Subway: Walnut-Locust. Map p 100.

★ **Caribou Café** CENTER CITY *FRENCH* This friendly, well-located brasserie is known for its steak frites, cassoulet, goat cheese salad, and wine list. 1126 Walnut St. (btw. 11th & 12th sts.) ☎ 215/625-9535. www.cariboucafe.com. Entrees $10–$29. AE, MC, V. Lunch & dinner daily. Bus: 9, 21, 23, 42. Map p. 100.

★★★ **Chifa** WASHINGTON SQUARE *PERUVIAN-CANTONESE* Artful tapas-style versions of ceviche, dim sum, empanadas, and hot pots meld diverse cuisines in a sexy, modern setting. 707 Chestnut St. (btw. 7th & 8th sts.) ☎ 215/925-5555. www.chifarestaurant.com. Plates $7–$31. AE, DC, DISC, MC, V. Dinner daily. Bus: 9, 21, 38, 42, 47. Subway: 8th St. Map p 100.

★ **City Tavern** OLD CITY *AMERICAN* The replica of the pub where

Bistro 7 is a local French favorite.

Costumed waiters add to the Colonial vibe of City Tavern, where America's forefathers met informally during Continental Congresses.

Washington and Adams knocked back mead and pepper-pot soup features Colonial-garbed servers, Martha Washington's turkey potpie, and Jefferson's home brew. *138 S. 2nd St. (at Walnut St.).* ☎ *215/413-1443. www.citytavern.com. Entrees $18–$35. AE, DISC, MC, V. Lunch & dinner daily. Bus: 21, 42. Subway: 2nd St. Map p 100.*

★ **kids Continental** OLD CITY *MODERN INTERNATIONAL* This chrome diner has something for everyone—from grilled cheese to Thai curry lobster and sugary martinis. (Elder sibling to below.) *138 Market St. (at 2nd St.).* ☎ *215/923-6069. www.continentalmartinibar. com. Entrees $12–$25. AE, DC, MC, V. Lunch & dinner daily. Bus: 5, 17, 33, 48. Subway: 2nd St. Map p 100.*

★ **kids Continental Mid-Town** RITTENHOUSE *MODERN INTERNATIONAL* Seats that swing and cocktails that buzz are the hallmarks of this three-floor lounge. Order a big salad and Szechuan shoestring fries. *1801 Chestnut St. (at 18th St.).* ☎ *215/567-1800. www.continental midtown.com. Entrees $8–$25. AE,*

DC, MC, V. Lunch & dinner daily. Bus: 9, 21, 42. Map p 100.

★ **Cosmi's Deli** SOUTH PHILLY *CHEESESTEAKS* Looks like a bodega, delivers like a champion: This neighbor to Pat's and Geno's has bested the big guys in taste tests time after time. *1501 S. 8th St. (at Dickinson St.).* ☎ *215/468-6093. www.cosmideli.com. Steaks $6–$9. AE, DISC, MC, V. Lunch & dinner daily. Bus: 47. Map p 99.*

★ **kids Devil's Alley** RITTEN-HOUSE *AMERICAN* A casual, popular spot for BBQ sliders, ribs, Cobb salad, creative burgers, and cold beers. *1907 Chestnut St. (btw. 19th & 20th sts.).* ☎ *215/751-0707. www.devilsalleybarandgrill.com. $9–$25. AE, DISC, DC, MC, V. Lunch & dinner Mon–Fri; brunch & dinner Sat–Sun. Bus: 9, 17, 21, 42. Map p 100.*

★★ **Dimitri's** QUEEN VILLAGE *GREEK BYOB* Seated elbow-to-elbow, locals dig into grilled squid, fresh bluefish, amazing hummus, and rice pudding; worth the first-come first-served wait. *795 S. 3rd St. (at Catharine St.).* ☎ *215/625-0556. Entrees $10–$20. No credit cards. Dinner daily. Bus: 57. Map p 99.*

Continental has an exceptionally diverse menu.

Chinatown

The country's fourth-largest Chinatown (just north of the Convention Center, btw. 9th & 11th sts., Arch & Vine sts.) represents many more populations and cultures than just Chinese; a few bustling blocks boast residents and businesses from Vietnam, Burma, Thailand, Korea, Japan, Malaysia, and beyond. Check out the four suspended 1,500-lb. bronze dragons at 9th and Arch streets, the Friendship Arch at 10th and Arch streets, and (of course) a vibrant, morning-to-late-night dining scene. Among more than 100 restaurants are daytime dim sum palaces **Ocean Harbor** (1023 Race St.; ☎ 215/574-1398) and **Dim Sum Garden** (59 N. 11th St.; ☎ 215/627-0218), and for non-carnivores, **Singapore Kosher Vegetarian Restaurant** (1006 Race St.; ☎ 215/922-3288; www.singapore vegetarian.com). For quick, inexpensive snacks in the form of bubble tea, red bean buns, and mango shakes, seek out **St. Honore** (935 Race St.; ☎ 215/925-5298) and **KC's Pastries** (109 N. 10th St.; ☎ 215/238-8808; www.kcpastries.com). This is definitely an area to explore by foot, as car traffic is almost always clogged in this centrally located neighborhood.

★★ **kids Distrito** UNIVERSITY CITY *MODERN MEXICAN* Mexico City yum and fun: neon booths, private karaoke, *lucha libre* wrestling masks, and fancied-up *taquería* fare. *3945 Chestnut St. (at 40th St.). ☎ 215/222-1657. www.distrito restaurant.com. Entrees $8–$55. AE, DISC, MC, V. Lunch Mon–Fri; dinner daily. Bus: 21, 30, 40. Subway: 40th St. Map p 100.*

★ **El Vez** CENTER CITY *MODERN MEXICAN* Made-to-order guac and margaritas that rock keep this colorful spot busy night after night in a lounge-y Mexi-Vegas atmosphere. *121 S. 13th St. (at Sansom St.). ☎ 215/928-9800. www.elvez restaurant.com. Entrees $10–$24. AE, DISC, MC, V. Lunch & dinner daily. Bus: 9, 12, 21, 38, 42, 124. Subway: Walnut-Locust or 13th St. Map p 100.*

★ **kids Famous Fourth Street Delicatessen** SOUTH STREET *JEWISH DELI* Order pastrami

sandwiches thick as phone books, matzo balls big as grapefruit, or marble cake that could double as a checkerboard. *700 S. 4th St. (at Bainbridge St.). ☎ 215/922-3274. Also at 38 S. 19th St. (at Ranstead St.). ☎ 215/568-3271. www.famous 4thstreetdelicatessen.com. Entrees $6–$27. AE, MC, V. Breakfast, lunch & dinner daily. Bus: 40, 57. Map p 100.*

★ **Farmicia** OLD CITY *MODERN AMERICAN* This bakery-owned restaurant has super-fresh, sustainably grown fare. Great for brunch. *15 S. 3rd St. (btw. Market & Chestnut sts.) ☎ 215/627-6274. www.farmicia restaurant.com. Entrees $16–$29. AE, MC, V. Lunch & dinner Tues–Fri; Breakfast, brunch & dinner Sat–Sun. Bus: 17, 33, 48, 57. Subway: 2nd St. Map p 100.*

★★★ **Fork** OLD CITY *CONTINENTAL* Fresh ingredients—Cape May fluke, house-made sausage, spring rhubarb—shine at this softly lit neighborhood brasserie, a date-night favorite. *306 Market St.* ☎ 215/625-9425. www.fork restaurant.com. *Entrees $16–$40. AE, DC, DISC, MC, V. Lunch & dinner Mon–Fri; dinner Sat; brunch & dinner Sun. Bus: 17, 33, 48, 57. Subway: 2nd St. Map p 100.*

★★★ Fountain Restaurant
LOGAN CIRCLE *INTERNATIONAL* The elegant Four Seasons hosts this tailored special-occasion affair, where service is king and Sunday brunch is to die for. *1 Logan Sq. (at 18th St.).* ☎ 215/963-1500. www. fourseasons.com/philadelphia. *Entrees $22–$60. AE, DC, MC, V. Breakfast & lunch daily; Dinner Tues– Sat. Bus: 2, 32, 33, 48. Map p 100.*

Geno's SOUTH PHILLY *CHEESE-STEAKS* Pat's across-the-street rival is bigger, brighter, and more controversial, thanks to its "This is America—when ordering speak English" policy. *1219 S. 9th St. (at E. Passyunk Ave.)* ☎ 215/389-0659. www.genosteaks.com. *Cheesesteaks $8–$10. No credit cards. Open 24 hr. Bus: 23, 47. Map p 99.*

★ Good Dog CENTER CITY *PUB FARE* Wooden booths, great microbrews, and a big-time jukebox are just background noise to a blue-cheese-stuffed burger that's the bomb. *224 S. 15th St. (btw. Walnut & Locust sts.).* ☎ 215/985-9600. www.gooddogbar.com. *Entrees $9–$21. AE, DC, DISC, MC, V. Lunch & dinner daily. Bus: 2, 9, 12, 21, 42. Subway: Walnut-Locust. Map p 100.*

★ HipCityVeg RITTENHOUSE *VEGAN/ASIAN* The excellent vegan fast-food cafe serves burgers, wraps, soups, and salads— largely locally sourced. Try the sweet potato fries and a signature Groothie (apple, banana, and kale smoothie). *127 S. 18th St. (btw. Sansom & Moravian sts.).* ☎ 215/278-7605. www.hipcityveg.com. *Entrees*

$9–$21. AE, DC, DISC, MC, V. Lunch & dinner daily. Bus: 9, 12, 21, 42. Subway: Walnut-Locust. Map p 100.

★ Jamonera CENTER CITY *SPANISH WINE BAR* Trendy eatery in a Spanish style for both classic and *nueva* tapas and *raciones*—jamon iberico and albondigas, but also clam chorizo. *105 S. 13th St. (btw. Chestnut & Sansom sts.).* ☎ 215/922-6061. www. jamonerarestaurant.com. *Tapas $7–$9; entrees $10–$24. AE, MC, V. Dinner daily. Bus: 9, 21, 38, 42, 124. Subway: Walnut-Locust or 13th St. Map p 100.*

★ Jim's Steaks SOUTH STREET CHEESESTEAKS The friendlier uptown cousin to Pat's and Geno's (started by the son of Jim's founder) won't balk if you ask for lettuce and tomato. Plus: indoor seating—and beer. *400 South St. (at 4th St.)* ☎ 215/928-1911. www.jimssteaks. com. *Cheesesteaks $7–$10. No credit cards. Lunch & dinner daily. Bus: 40, 57. Map p 100.*

kids Jones OLD CITY *AMERICAN COMFORT* Just what the family ordered: mac and cheese, glazed carrots, meatloaf, and chicken nachos in a *Brady Bunch*–retro sunken dining room. *700 Chestnut St. (at 7th St.).* ☎ 215/223-5663. www.jones-restaurant.com. *AE, DC, MC, V. Entrees $9–$23. Lunch & dinner daily. Bus: 9, 21, 38, 42, 47. Subway: 8th St. Map p 100.*

★ Kanella WASHINGTON SQUARE *GREEK BYOB* From the island of Cyprus, this place offers rustic (goat stew) and Mediterranean (pasta with capers and mint) fare. *1001 Spruce St. (at 10th St.).* ☎ 215/922-1773. www.kanella restaurant.com. *Entrees $21–$32. DISC, MC, V. Lunch Fri–Sat; dinner Tues–Sat; light dinner Sun. Bus: 12, 23. Map p 100.*

The burgers at Good Dog are legendary.

★★★ **Lacroix** RITTENHOUSE
MODERN INTERNATIONAL
Overlooking the Square. Each gracious meal seems more elegant than the last. A la carte at lunch; dinners are 4- or 8-course tasting menus. *The Rittenhouse Hotel, 210 W. Rittenhouse (btw. Locust & Walnut sts.). 215/546-9000. www.lacroix restaurant.com. AE, DC, DISC, MC, V. Entrees $16–$25; dinner menus: $75–$120. Breakfast, lunch & dinner daily. Bus: 9, 12, 17, 21, 42. Map p 100.*

★ **Lee How Fook** CHINATOWN
CHINESE BYOB Garlicky good-for-you greens, hearty duck noodle soup, and salt-baked squid pack this family joint night after night. *219 N. 11th St. (btw. Race & Vine sts.). 215/925-7266. www.leehow fook.com. Entrees $7–$16. MC, V. Lunch & dinner Tues–Sun. Bus: 23, 61. Map p 100.*

★★ **Lolita** CENTER CITY *MODERN MEXICAN BYOB* Classic dishes get dressed up for a night on the town at this funky little spot. Bring your own tequila for fresh-fruit margaritas. *106 S. 13th St. (btw. Sansom & Chestnut sts.). 215/546-7100. www.lolitabyob.com. Entrees $18–$24. No credit cards. Dinner daily. Bus: 9, 21, 38, 42, 124. Subway: Walnut-Locust or 13th St. Map p 100.*

★ **Tequila's** RITTENHOUSE
UPSCALE MEXICAN Classic fare, snappy delivery, and smooth tequilas served up in a mural-covered mansion. *1602 Locust St. (btw. 16th & 17th sts.). 215/546-0181. www.tequilasphilly.com. Entrees $15–$24. AE, DC, MC, V. Lunch Mon–Fri; dinner daily. Bus: 2, 12. Map p 100.*

★ **Marra's** EAST PASSYUNK *ITALIAN/PIZZA* One meal at this no-nonsense eatery, with its sublimely simple pies and homemade escarole soup, and you'll never eat at Pizza Hut again. *1734 E. Passyunk Ave. (between Morris & Moore sts.). 215/463-9249. www.marrasone.com. Entrees $6.50–$19. DISC, MC, V. Lunch & dinner Tues–Sat; dinner Sun. Bus: 23, 29. Subway: Tasker-Morris. Map p 99.*

★★ **Melograno** RITTENHOUSE
MODERN ITALIAN BYOB House-cured pancetta, fig and walnut stuffing, home-made pappardelle: This ever-bustling bistro offers Roman fare for modern times. *2012 Sansom St. (btw. 20th & 21st sts.). 215/875-8116. www.melograno restaurant.com. Entrees $16–$33. MC, V. Dinner Tues–Sun. Bus: 9, 12, 17, 21, 42. Map p 100.*

★★ **Mercato** CENTER CITY
MODERN ITALIAN BYOB This glittering, no-reservations (except pre-theater) bistro makes every meal feel like a dinner party—only with better short ribs and risotto than you could ever pull off at home. *1216 Spruce St. (at Camac St.). 215/985-2962. www.mercato byob.com. Entrees $20–$30. No credit cards. Dinner daily. Bus: 12, 23. Subway: Walnut-Locust. Map p 100*

★★ **Meritage** RITTENHOUSE
MODERN FUSION This corner spot has the three essential elements of a romantic bistro: cozy

Midtown's Mercato has an inviting atmosphere alongside great food.

environs, ample wine list, and cheese platters. The 4-course vegan tasting menu is unexpected. *500 S. 20th St. (at Lombard St.)* ☎ *215/985-1922. www.meritage philadelphia.com. Entrees $12–$26. AE, DISC, MC, V. Dinner Tues–Sat. Bus: 17, 40. Map p 100.*

★ **The Mildred** BELLA VISTA *MODERN AMERICAN* Seasonal New American cuisine made with locally sourced ingredients—from haute steak and potatoes to fiddle-head fern rice to beer-braised mussels—from chef Michael Santoro in a chic jewel box. *824 S. 8th St. (btw. Catharine & Christian sts.).* ☎ *267/ 687-1600. www.the-mildred.com. Entrees $18–$28. AE, DC, MC, V. Dinner Tues–Sun; brunch Sat–Sun. Bus: 47. Map p 99.*

★★ **Morimoto** OLD CITY *JAPANESE* The Iron Chef's signature flash in an aptly futuristic showplace. Splurge on tableside-made tofu, luscious toro, and a sake martini. *723 Chestnut St. (btw. 7th & 8th sts.).* ☎ *215/413-9070. www.morimoto restaurant.com. Entrees $26–$49. AE, DC, MC, V. Lunch Mon–Fri; dinner daily. Bus: 9, 21, 38, 42, 47. Subway: 8th St. Map p 100.*

★ **Nineteen** BROAD STREET *CONTINENTAL* On the Bellevue's 19th floor, giant pearls drip from ceilings where formal tea, fresh oysters, and dress-up dinners are served. *Park Hyatt, 200 S. Broad St. (at Walnut St.).* ☎ *215/790-1919. www.nineteenrestaurant.com. Entrees $18–$45. AE, DC, DISC, MC, V. Breakfast, lunch & dinner daily. Bus: 4, 9, 12, 21, 27, 32, 42. Subway: Walnut-Locust. Map p 100.*

★★★ **Osteria** NORTH BROAD *ITALIAN* It's worth the trek to North Broad for gourmet Italian fare. Jeff Michaud won the 2010 James Beard for Best Chef Mid-Atlantic with dishes such as egg-topped pizza and wild boar Bolognese. Book ahead. *640 N. Broad St. (at Wallace St.).* ☎ *215/ 763-0920. www.osteriaphilly.com. Entrees $15–$36. AE, DC, MC, V. Lunch Thurs–Fri; dinner daily. Bus: 4, 16, 61. Subway: Spring Garden St or Fairmount. Map p 100.*

★★ **The Oyster House** RITTEN-HOUSE *AMERICAN SEAFOOD* Everything that swims (and is classic), including oysters opened by shuckers who've been at it for decades. *1516 Sansom St. (btw. 15th & 16th sts.).* ☎ *215/567-7683. www. oysterhousephilly.com. Entrees $14–$33. AE, DISC, MC, V. Lunch & dinner Mon–Sat; dinner Sun. Bus: 2, 9, 12, 21, 42. Subway: Walnut-Locust or 15th St. Map p 100.*

★★ **Parc** RITTENHOUSE *FRENCH* Classic Parisian bistro fare in a see-and-be-seen setting. Homemade bread, coq au vin, steak au poivre, and quiet breakfasts are standouts. *227 S. 18th St. (at Locust St.).* ☎ *215/545-2262. www.parc-restaurant.com. Entrees $13–$33. AE, DC, MC, V. Breakfast, lunch & dinner Mon–Fri; brunch, lunch, dinner Sat–Sun. Bus: 9, 12, 21, 42. Map p 100.*

★★ **Paradiso** EAST PASSYUNK *ITALIAN* Swanked-out South Philly neighbors nibble smoked trout salads and airy fried calamari before tucking into rabbit cacciatore and olive-dressed ahi tuna. *1627 E. Passyunk Ave. (between Tasker & Morris sts.).* ☎ *215/271-2066. www. paradisophilly.com. Entrees $18–$24. AE, MC, V. Lunch Tues–Fri; dinner Tues–Sun. Bus: 23, 29. Subway: Tasker-Morris. Map p 99.*

★ **Pat's King of Steaks** SOUTH PHILLY *CHEESESTEAKS* The originator, in all its roadside glory. Order one "wid" onions and/or (Cheez) Whiz. *1237 E. Passyunk Ave. (at 9th & Wharton sts.).* ☎ *215/468-1546. www.patskingofsteaks.com. Cheesesteaks $7–$9.50. No credit cards. Open 24 hr. Bus: 23, 47. Map p 99.*

★★ **Pizzeria Stella** SOCIETY HILL *PIZZA* This place offers thin-crust, cleverly topped (guanciale, pistachios) pies, plus juice glasses of Prosecco, egg-topped asparagus, and olive oil gelato. *420 S. 2nd St. (at Lombard St.).* ☎ *215/320-8000. www.pizzeriastella.net. Pizzas $11–$19. AE, DISC, MC, V. Lunch & dinner daily. Bus: 12, 40, 57. Map p 100.*

★★ **Pumpkin** RITTENHOUSE *AMERICAN BYOB* Little and locavore, this minimalist, homey neighborhood gem excels at seasonal cuisine, seafood, and steak. (Reservations highly recommended.) *1713 South St. (btw. 17th & 18th sts.).* ☎ *215/545-4448. www.pumpkin philly.com. Entrees $26–$27. No*

Osteria's menu features gourmet Italian comfort food.

credit cards. Dinner Tues–Sun. Bus: 2, 40. Map p 100.

Ralph's Italian Restaurant BELLA VISTA *ITALIAN* Meatballs and "red gravy" (marinara), chicken Sorrento, and unpretentious service are staples at this century-old family trattoria. *760 S. 9th St. (between Fitzwater & Catharine sts.).* ☎ *215/627-6011. www.ralphsrestaurant.com. Entrees $11–$32. No credit cards. Lunch & dinner daily. Bus: 47m, 47. Map p 99.*

★ **Rangoon** CHINATOWN BURMESE If you've never had the pleasure of digging into a tealeaf salad, coconut rice, or 1,000-layer bread, do it at this casual, women-run spot. *112 N. 9th St. (btw. Arch & Cherry sts.).* ☎ *215/829-8939. www. rangoonrestaurant.com. Entrees $7–$19. MC, V. Lunch & dinner daily. Bus: 47m, 48, 61. Map p 100*

★★★ **Reading Terminal Market** CENTER CITY *MARKET* This 114-year-old farmers' market and eatery emporium in the old train station near the convention center has food stands offering everything from Amish to Indian, soul food to kebabs, cajun to cheesesteaks... and Bassett's ice cream. *51 N. 12th St. (btw. Arch & Filbert sts.).* ☎ *215/922-2317. www.readingterminal market.org. Dishes $3–$25. Open 8am–6pm Mon–Sat; 9am–5pm Sun.*

The Oyster House boasts some of the best shuckers around.

Some accept credit cards. Bus: 17, 23, 33, 38, 44, 48, 62. Subway: 11 St. Map p 100.

★★ Rouge RITTENHOUSE

AMERICAN-FRENCH In the mood for a lavish burger, a teensy salad, or a bottle of Dom for lunch? This luxe little bistro understands—as long as you're wearing your good jewelry. *205 S. 18th St. (btw. Walnut & Locust sts.).* ☎ *215/732-6622. www.rouge98.com. Entrees $14–$33. AE, DISC, MC, V. Lunch & dinner daily; brunch Sat–Sun. Bus: 9, 12, 21, 42. Map p 100.*

Sabrina's BELLA VISTA *AMERI-CAN BYOB* The reason folks wait hours for a seat in this pink-and-blue-hued eatery? Must be something in the humongous French toast. *910 Christian St. (btw. 9th & 10th sts.).* ☎ *215/574-1599. www. sabrinascafe.com. Entrees $6–$13. AE, MC, V. Breakfast & lunch daily. Bus: 23, 47m. Map p 99.*

★ kids Sam's Morning Glory Diner BELLA VISTA *AMERICAN*

"Be nice or leave" is the motto of this corner luncheonette, where ketchup is homemade, coffee comes in steel mugs, and frittatas and pancakes are worth the wait. *735 S. 10th St. (at Fitzwater St.).* ☎ *215/413-3999. $5–$11. No credit cards. Breakfast & lunch daily. Bus: 23, 47m. Map p 99.*

★★ Southwark SOUTH STREET

CONTINENTAL The ultimate spot to eat is at the bar, from your first Manhattan to your last bite of rosemary panna cotta. Late-night light menu, too. *701 S. 4th St (at Bainbridge St.).* ☎ *215/238-1888. www. southwarkrestaurant.com. Entrees $17–$25. AE, MC, V. Dinner Tues–Sat; brunch Sun. Bus: 40, 57. Map p 100.*

★★ Supper SOUTH STREET

MODERN AMERICAN Unexpected send-ups of comfort fare (latkes, cioppino, deviled eggs, pork BBQ) star at this chic brasserie, where the "Sunday supper" and happy hour deals are not to be missed. *926 South St.* ☎ *215/592-8180. www.supperphilly.com. AE, MC, V. $15–$29. Dinner daily; brunch Sat–Sun. Bus: 40, 47m. Map p 100.*

★★ Table 31 RITTENHOUSE

AMERICAN A snazzy, suit-and-tie steakhouse in the Comcast Center. Forget platinum; bring the titanium card. *1701 JFK Blvd. (at 17th St.).* ☎ *215/567-7111. www.table-31. com. Entrees $14–$46. AE, DC, MC, V. Lunch & dinner Mon–Fri; dinner Sat. Bus: 2, 27, 32, 48. Subway: 15th St. Map p 100.*

★★ Tinto RITTENHOUSE

BASQUE TAPAS Chef Garces' cozy lounge offers delicious snacks like Serrano-wrapped figs and cockle-studded sea bass. *114 S. 20th St. (btw. Sansom & Chestnut sts.).* ☎ *215/665-9150. www.tinto restaurant.com. Plates $4–$21. AE, DC, MC, V. Dinner daily; brunch Sun. Bus: 9, 12, 17, 21, 42. Map p 100.*

★★ Tony Luke's Roast Pork

SOUTH PHILLY *ITALIAN SAND-WICHES* Neon-lit, two-handed dining: Have the roast pork with garlicky broccoli rabe and sharp provolone. *39 E. Oregon Ave. (btw. I-95. & Front St.).* ☎ *215/551-5725. www.tonylukes.com. Entrees $6–$10. No credit cards. Lunch & dinner daily; breakfast Mon–Sat. Bus: G, 7, 57. Map p 99.*

★ **Valanni** CENTER CITY *MEDITERRANEAN-LATIN TAPAS* Enjoy the modern lounge vibe, spicy-sweet snacks (bacon-wrapped blue cheese-stuffed figs, chickpea frites), and paella meant for sharing. Late-night menu to 1am. *1229 Spruce St. (btw. 12th & 13th sts.).* ☎ *215/790-9494. www.valanni.com. Entrees $15–$26. AE, DISC, MC, V. Dinner daily; brunch Sat–Sun. Bus: 12, 23. Subway: Walnut-Locust. Map p 100.*

★★★ **Vetri** CENTER CITY *ITALIAN* Bon Appetit and Esquire have both christened chef Marc Vetri's brownstone eatery the best Italian restaurant in the U.S. (Mario Batali was only willing to go "Best on the East Coast.") Tasting menus only. *1312 Spruce St. (btw. 13th & Juniper sts.).* ☎ *215/732-3478. www.vetriristorante.com. Tasting menu $155. AE, MC, V. Dinner Mon–Sat. Bus: 4, 23, 27, 32. Subway: Walnut-Locust. Map p 100.*

★ **Victor Café** SOUTH PHILLY *ITALIAN* Giant veal chops and homemade pastas compete for fame with this trattoria's opera-singing servers. Fun fact: This was the retired champ's restaurant "Adrian's: in 2006's *Rocky Balboa. 1303 Dickinson St. (btw. 13th & Broad sts.).* ☎ *215/468-3040. www.victorcafe.com. AE, MC, V. Main courses $16–$36. AE, MC, V. Dinner daily. Bus: 4, 23, 29. Subway: Tasker-Morris. Map p 99.*

★ **Vietnam** CHINATOWN *VIETNAMESE* Peanut-dusted rice vermicelli, charbroiled pork, lime-glazed chicken, and handsome surroundings make this gently exotic spot popular with the neighbors. *221 N. 11th St. (btw. Race & Vine sts.).* ☎ *215/592-1163. www.eatatvietnam.com. Entrees $10–$15. AE, DISC, MC, V. Lunch & dinner daily. Bus: 23, 61. Map p 100.*

★ **Villa di Roma** ITALIAN MARKET *ITALIAN* Extra casual Italian-American fare including classic meatballs, fried asparagus, and homemade gnocchi is served in a red-brick-tiled space. *936 S. 9th St. (btw. Montrose & Carpenter sts.).* ☎ *215/592-1295. Entrees $11–$30. No credit cards. Lunch & dinner Fri–Sat; dinner Sun–Thurs. Bus: 47, 47m, 64. Map p 99.*

★★★ **Village Whiskey** RITTENHOUSE *GOURMET PUB* Find Philly's longest whiskey list (and longer barstool wait) and a burger

The menu at Southwark is as high-class as the surroundings.

that'll knock you off that hard-won seat. *118 S. 20th St. (at Sansom St.).* ☎ *215/665-1088. www.village whiskey.com. Entrees $10–$26. AE, DISC, MC, V. Lunch & dinner daily. Bus: 9, 12, 17, 21, 42. Map p 100.*

★ Water Works Restaurant
FAIRMOUNT *AMERICAN/ GREEK* This restaurant is so pretty, with history, a view, grilled specialties, and a gourmet H2O menu. *640 Waterworks Dr. (btw. Philadelphia Museum of Art & Boathouse Row).* ☎ *215/ 236-9000. www.thewaterworks restaurant.com. Entrees $19–$37. AE, DC, DISC, MC, V. Lunch & dinner Tues–Sat; brunch Sun. Bus: 32, 38, 43. Map p 100.*

★★ Xochitl
SOCIETY HILL *MODERN MEXICAN* Distinctive, refined, understated, and lounge-y, the fare and the vibe at sleek "So-cheet" are refreshingly sophisticated. *408 S. 2nd St. (btw. Pine & Lombard sts.).* ☎ *215/238-7280. www.xochitlphilly.com. Entrees $13–$26. AE, DISC, MC, V. Dinner daily. Bus: 12, 40, 57. Map p 100.*

★★★ Zahav
OLD CITY/SOCIETY HILL *ISRAELI* Fans swear by the rich hummus and savory kebabs. *237 St. James Place. (btw. 2nd & 3rd*

The hummus and kebabs at Zahav have a legion of fans.

sts. at Dock St.). ☎ *215/625-8800. www.zahavrestaurant.com. Plates $7–$20. AE, DISC, MC, V. Dinner daily. Bus: 12, 21, 42, 57. Subway: 2nd St. Map p 100.*

★ Zento
OLD CITY *JAPANESE BYOB* Tiny but mighty, this friendly spot offers stellar staples and clever square maki, plus excellent teriyaki and tempura for the sushi-shy. *132 Chestnut St. (btw. Front & 2nd sts.).* ☎ *215/925-9998. www.zentocontemporary.com. Entrees $16–$37. AE, MC, V. Lunch & dinner Mon–Sat; dinner Sun. Bus: 21, 42. Subway: 2nd St. Map p 100.* ●

Nightlife Best Bets

Best Beer List
★★ Monk's Café, 264 S. 16th St.
(p 121)

Best Dive Bar
★ Dirty Frank's, 347 S. 13th St.
(p 118)

Best for Local Brews
★★★ Standard Tap, 901 N. 2nd
St. (p 122)

Best for Canoodling
★ Friday Saturday Sunday, 261 S.
21st St. (p 122)

Best for Eating
★★ Pub and Kitchen, 1946 Lombard St. (p 118)

Best for a Long-Term
Relationship
★★ Swann Lounge at the Four
Seasons, 1 Logan Square (p 120)

Best for Martinis
★★ Nineteen Bar, 200 S. Broad St.
(p 120)

Best for Bowling
★ North Bowl, 909 N. 2nd St.
(p 115)

Best for Salsa Dancing
Brasil's, 112 Chestnut St. (p 115)

Best Irish Pub
★★ Fergie's, 1214 Sansom St.
(p 121)

Best Classic Gay Bar
★ Tavern on Camac, 243 S. Camac
St. (p 119)

Best for Dancing
Devotion/Shampoo, 417 N. 8th St.
(p 118)

Monk's Café has the city's best beer list. Previous page: Nineteen Bar is renowned for its martinis.

Nightlife in Northern Liberties

700 **6**
Bar Ferdinand **3**
Devotion/Shampoo **1**
North Bowl **4**
Silk City **2**
Standard Tap **5**

Nightlife A to Z

Bowling

Lucky Strike Lanes CENTER CITY This swank, overpriced chain alley has 24 lanes, two floors, a low-slung lounge, cocktails, buckets of beers, and sliders galore. *1336 Chestnut St. (btw. 13th & Broad sts.).* ☎ 215/545-2471. www.bowllucky strike.com. *$45–$55 per hr. lane rate plus $6–$7 per person per game. Shoe rental $4.60. Bus: 4, 9, 21, 27, 32, 38, 42, 124. Subway: Walnut-Locust or 13th St. Map p 116.*

★ **North Bowl** NORTHERN LIB-ERTIES This retro-chic, locally owned alley has 17 lanes, two bars (corn dogs and local brews), and a major local following. *909 N. 2nd St.* (btw. Poplar & N. Hancock sts.). ☎ 215/238-2695. www.northbowl philly.com. *$5–$6 per person per game. Shoe rental $5. Bus: 5, 57. Sub-way: Spring Garden St. Map p 115.*

Dance Clubs

Brasil's OLD CITY This compact upstairs club serves up the hottest Latin groove scene (and coolest caipirinhas) in town. Free salsa lessons from 9 to 10:30pm on Wednesday, Friday, and Saturday nights. *112 Chestnut St. (btw. Front & 2nd sts.).* ☎ 215/413-1700. www. brasilsnightclub-philly.com. *Cover $5–$10. Bus: 5, 17, 21, 38, 42. Sub-way: 2nd St. Map p 116.*

Nightlife in Center City

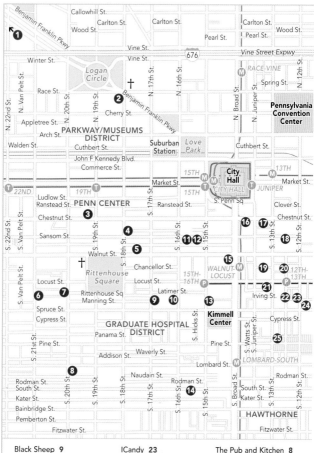

M	SEPTA Subway
P	PATCO Light Rail
T	Trolley
†	Church
✡	Synagogue
▣	Point of Interest
✉	Post Office

The elegant L'Etage offers the occasional cabaret act.

D'Angelo's Lounge RITTEN-HOUSE   Like a party scene from *The Sopranos*, this trattoria-with-a-dance-floor caters to a mature crowd who groove to Sinatra and Miami Sound Machine. *256 S. 20th St. (at Rittenhouse Square St. btw. Locust & Spruce sts.).* ☎ *215/546-3935. www.dangeloristorante.com. No cover. Bus: 12, 17. Map p 116.*

Devotion/Shampoo NORTHERN LIBERTIES   Formerly "Shampoo," a thumping maze of all things to all clubbers: three floors and eight bars with Goth, 80s, drag, hip-hop—even, some Sunday afternoons, toddler disco (www.baby lovesdisco.com). *417 N. 8th St. (on Willow, btw. Callowhill & Spring Garden sts.).* ☎ *215/922-7500. www. devotionnightclub.com. Cover $5–$25. Bus: 47, 47m, 61. Map p 115.*

The Ten Six Club RITTEN-HOUSE   A new club in an old space above Alfa restaurant, with karaoke Tuesdays, Brit-rock Wednesdays, indie-dance-house Thursdays, and on the weekends (cover $5–$10) '80s pop and top 40. *1709 Walnut St. (btw. 17th & 18th sts.).* ☎ *215/751-0201. www.tensix club.com. Cover $0–$10. Bus: 2, 9, 12, 21, 42. Map p 116.*

Dine-In Bars

★★ Bar Ferdinand NORTHERN LIBERTIES   Sangria; $2 wine specials; and tapas of smoked fish, curried ham, and spiced almonds star at this artsy spot. Tabs here can add up fast. *1030 N. 2nd St. (btw. W. Wildey & W. George sts.).* ☎ *215/ 923-1313. www.barferdinand.com. No cover. Bus: 5. Subway: Spring Garden St. Map p 115.*

★★ The Pub and Kitchen RIT-TENHOUSE   Rustic and refined, this corner spot has the menu of a bistro and the vibe of a stylish bar. Expect waits on weekends (no reservations). *1946 Lombard St. (at 20th St.).* ☎ *215/545-0350. www.thepub andkitchen.com. No cover. Bus: 17, 40. Map p 116.*

Dive Bars

★ Bob & Barbara's SOUTH STREET   This retro-style spot comes replete with vintage beer ads and lighting, $3 Jim Beam shots, PBR can specials, and, on Thursday night, drag performances. *1509 South St. (btw. 15th & 16th sts.).* ☎ *215/545-4511. www. bobandbarbaras.com. No cover. Bus: 2, 40. Map p 116.*

★ Dirty Frank's CENTER CITY No sign, just a portrait mural of famous "Franks" announces this more-shabby-than-chic watering hole dating back to Prohibition. Locals play darts and sink into booths. Order a bottle, not a pint. *347 S. 13th St. (at Pine St.).* ☎ *215/ 732-5010. www.dirtyfranksbar.com. No cover. Bus: 4, 23, 27, 32, 40. Map p 116.*

McGlinchey's RITTENHOUSE Ms. Pac Man tables, grumpy bartenders, 25-cent hotdogs, cheap shots, and even cheaper beer; no wonder this place is where the down-and-out chill and the glamorous slum. A proud exemption from Philly's smoke-free laws. *259 S. 15th St. (btw. Locust & Spruce sts.).* ☎ *215/735-1259. www.mcglincheys. com. No cover. Bus: 2, 4, 12, 27, 32. Subway: Walnut-Locust. Map p 116.*

Oscar's Tavern RITTENHOUSE The textbook spot to hide from the boss, this dirt-cheap place dodged the smoking ban, allowing patrons to light up later into the night. Don't fear the roast beef. *1524 Sansom St. (btw. 15th & 16th sts.).* ☎ *215/972-9938. No cover. Bus: 2, 9, 12, 21, 42. Map p 116.*

★ **Ray's Happy Birthday Bar** SOUTH PHILLY Lou runs this corner joint (recently discovered by irony-dealing hipsters) and will be seriously bummed if you don't call ahead to tell him it's your b-day. Open at 7am(!), it's the best place to go for a brew after a cheesesteak at Pat's or Geno's. *1200 Passyunk Ave. (at Federal St.).* ☎ *215/365-1169. www.thehappy birthdaybar.com. No cover. Bus: 47, 47m. Map p 116.*

Gay Bars

Sisters CENTER CITY The only lesbian bar in town covers 5,000 square feet to satisfy a diverse group that ranges from buzz-cut to glam. Best nights: Thursday's karaoke and Saturday's singles dance party. *No credit cards. 1320 Chancellor St. (btw. 13th & Juniper sts., Walnut & Locust sts.).* ☎ *215/ 735-0735. www.sistersnightclub.com. Cover $0–$10. Bus: 9, 12, 21, 42. Subway: Walnut-Locust. Map p 116.*

★ **Tavern on Camac** CENTER CITY This friendly, 60-year-old piano bar tucked on a side street is one of the oldest gay pubs in the U.S. Something for any mood: Dining in the basement; piano bar on the ground floor; dance club upstairs. *243 S. Camac St. (btw. 12th & 13th sts., Locust & Spruce sts.).* ☎ *215/545-0900. www.tavernon camac.com. No cover. Bus: 12, 23. Map p 116.*

ICandy CENTER CITY Three floors of gay partying (lesbians are the focus on Temptress Tuesdays), with a pub on the ground floor, dance club on the second floor, and lounge on the top floor that spills onto the roof deck in summer. Skews younger. *254 S. 12th St. (btw. Locust & Spruce sts.).* ☎ *267/324-3500. www.clubicandy.com. Cover $0–$10. Bus: 23. Map p 116.*

★ **Voyeur** CENTER CITY There's room for 1,000 among the lavishly decorated floors (red velvet, crystal spangles, faux fur), home to some of the East Coast's best DJs—and Philly's biggest circuit parties. Drag queens serve cocktails. *1221 St. James St. (btw. 12th & 13th sts.).* ☎ *215/735-5772. www.voyeurnight club.com. Cover $7–$25. Bus: 9, 12, 21, 23, 42. Map p 116.*

Woody's CENTER CITY This mega-bar has anchored the gayborhood since the '70s, sort of a community center with booze. Among the umpteen theme nights: Latin, country two-step, karaoke, and college. *202 S. 13th St. (btw. Walnut & Locust sts.).* ☎ *215/545-1893. www.woodysbar.com. Cover* free–$10. Bus: 9, 12, 21, 42. Map p 116.

Lounges

★ **L'Etage** SOUTH STREET Above Beau Monde (see p 116), this elegant spot offers banquette seating, a nice wine list, and entertainment from poetry slams to cabaret to weekend DJs. *624 S. 6th St. (at Bainbridge St.).* ☎ *215/592-0656. www.creperie-beaumonde.com. Cover $0–$15. Bus: 40, 47. Map p 116.*

★★ **Nineteen Bar** CENTER CITY Known for its fireside coziness, this 19th-floor lounge, bar, and restaurant is nonetheless see-and-be-seen, with an impeccable crowd—and martinis to match. *Park Hyatt at the Bellevue, 200 S. Broad St. (at Walnut St.).* ☎ *215/790-1919. www.nineteenrestaurant.com. No cover. Bus: 4, 9, 12, 21, 27, 32, 42. Subway: Walnut-Locust. Map p 116.*

700 NORTHERN LIBERTIES Early on, the crowd at this two-floor spot is hipper-than-thou (in a nice way) artistic-types. Later, it's a mixed bag of the same, plus bachelorettes, frat bros, and yuppies. *700 N. 2nd St. (at Fairmount Ave.).* ☎ *215/413-3181. www.the700.org. No cover. Bus: 5, 25. Subway: Spring Garden St. Map p 115.*

★ **Silk City** NORTHERN LIBERTIES The more dimly lit arm to a silver car diner and beer garden, this lounge is known for its hipster clientele and DJs. *435 Spring Garden St. (btw. 4th & 5th sts.).* ☎ *215/592-8838. www.silkcityphilly. com. Cover $0–$10. Bus: 43, 57. Map p 115.*

★★ **Swann Lounge at the Four Seasons** LOGAN CIRCLE There's something about perching in a cozy banquette, nibbling cheese straws, and sipping a top-dollar grapefruit martini that makes the day just seem better. *1 Logan Sq. (at 18th St.).* ☎ *215/963-1500. www.fourseasons.com. No cover. Bus: 2, 32, 33, 48. Map p 116.*

Taprooms

Black Sheep RITTENHOUSE A cozy Irish pub in a Colonial brick townhouse, popular among the suit-and-tie crowd. The menu's worthy of staying past happy hour, too. *247 S. 17th St. (at Latimer St.).* ☎ *215/545-9473. www.theblack sheeppub.com. No cover. Bus: 2, 12. Map p 116.*

★ **Bridgid's** FAIRMOUNT Tiny and friendly, this horseshoe-shaped bar stocks an impressive array of Belgian beers—best accompanied

North Bowl's retro design includes 17 lanes and two bars.

Silk City's beer garden is a must on warm summer nights.

by inexpensive dishes from the varied menu. *726 N. 24th St. (btw. Fairmount Ave & Aspen St.).* ☎ *215/232-3232. www.bridgids.com. No cover. Bus: 7, 48. Map p 116.*

Cavanaugh's SOCIETY HILL If it's 4am and a World Cup match is taking place, you can probably catch it at this Brit-inspired pub. In 2013 it became a gastropub in Philly's Cavanaugh's clan, putting Ken McNamara—the fondly remembered chef here from way back when this was "Dickens Inn"—in charge of the kitchen. *421 S. 2nd St. (btw. Pine & Lombard sts.).* ☎ *215/928-0232. www.cavsheadhouse.com. No cover. Bus: 40. Map p 116.*

Drinker's Tavern and Drinker's Pub OLD CITY and RITTENHOUSE Never have a pair of Philly bars been so aptly named. At either location, shotgun a PBR for a buck on Saturdays ($2 otherwise). *124 Market St. (btw. Front & 2nd sts.);* ☎ *215/351-0141. Bus: 5, 17, 21, 33, 42, 48. Subway: 2nd St. 1903 Chestnut St. (btw. 19th & 20th sts.);* ☎ *215/564-0914. www.drinkers215.com. No cover. Bus: 9, 17, 21, 42. Map p 116.*

★★ Fergie's CENTER CITY An Irish pub actually owned by an Irishman, this find is cozy and candlelit,

and offers a large list of brews complimented by some tasty potpies, burgers, and mussels and fries. *1214 Sansom St. (btw. 12th & 13th sts.).* ☎ *215/928-8118. www.fergies.com. No cover. Bus: 9, 12, 21, 38, 42, 124. Map p 116.*

★ McGillin's Olde Ale House CENTER CITY Hard to find—but worth it—Philadelphia's oldest continuously operating tavern is as popular now as its ever been, only now there's karaoke (Wed and Sun) with the pitchers of lager. *1310 Drury St. (btw. Chestnut & Sansom sts., 13th & Juniper sts.).* ☎ *215/735-5562. www.mcgillins.com. No cover. Bus: 9, 21, 38, 42, 124. Map p 116.*

★★ Monk's Cafe RITTENHOUSE For some reason, the Penn crowd has adopted this beer-connoisseur's spot, but you should go regardless of the elbow-throwing crowd, if only for the house's special Flemish sour ale (or a bucket of mussels and the house fries). *264 S. 16th St. (btw. Locust & Spruce sts.).* ☎ *215/545-7005. www.monkscafe.com. No cover. Bus: 2, 12. Map p 116.*

★ Nodding Head Brewery and Restaurant RITTENHOUSE For the ultimate locavore drinker: Six truly interesting beers brewed on premises, plus a nice, absorptive menu not unlike Monk's (see above). *1516 Sansom St. (btw. 15th & 16th sts.).* ☎ *215/569-9525. www. noddinghead.com. No cover. Bus: 2, 9, 12, 21, 42. Map p 116.*

★★★ Standard Tap NORTH-

ERN LIBERTIES   Twenty local—and only local—beers daily, plus whatever other kind of drink you require, are served at this hip, handsome, vast, and justly popular gastro-pub. If it's nice out, ask for a table on the deck. *901 N. 2nd St. (at Poplar St.).* ☎ *215/238-0630. www.standardtap. com. No cover. Bus: 5. Subway: Spring Garden St. Map p 115.*

Wine Bars

★ Friday Saturday Sunday's "Tank Bar" RITTENHOUSE

Above a neighborhood restaurant known for its retro cuisine, this romantic spot offers wines with the lowest (around 10%) markups in town. *261 S. 21st St. (btw. Locust & Spruce sts.).* ☎ *215/546-4232. www. frisatsun.com. No cover. Bus: 12, 17. Map p 116.*

★ Il Bar OLD CITY   Tucked into

the ground floor of the Penn's View Hotel (see p 116) are some 120 wines by the glass, available by flights of five 1.5-ounce pours—all part of the hotel's Italian restaurant. *14 N. Front St. (btw. Market & Church sts.).* ☎ *215/922-7600. www. pennsviewhotel.com. No cover. Bus: , 17, 21, 33, 42, 48. Subway: 2nd St. Map p 116.*

Il Bar offers more than 100 wines by the glass.

★★ Tria CENTER CITY, RITTEN-

HOUSE and WASHINGTON SQUARE WEST   This pair of narrow bars feels very Euro, what with their spare handsomeness, little savory plates, and beginner-friendly selection of vino, categorized as bubbly, bold, zippy, and so on. *Two locations: Rittenhouse: 123 S. 18th St. (at Sansom St.);* ☎ *215/972-8742. Bus: 9, 12, 21, 42. Washington Square West: 1137 Spruce St. (at 12th St.);* ☎ *215/629-9200. www.tria cafe.com. Bus: 23. Map p 116.* ●

Arts & Entertainment Best Bets

Best **Theater for Children's Performance**
★★ **kids** Arden Theatre Company, 40 S. 2nd St. (p 125)

Best for **Orchestra**
★★★ Kimmel Center for the Performing Arts, 300 S. Broad St. (p 129)

Best for **Local Productions**
★ **kids** Walnut Street Theater, 825 Walnut St. (p 128)

Best **Theater Facility, Period**
★★★ Academy of Music, 240 S. Broad St. (p 129)

Best **Hidden Gem**
★★ Academy of Vocal Arts, 1920 Spruce St. (p 129)

Best for **Outdoor Concerts**
★★ Mann Music Center, 5201 Parkside Ave. (p 130)

Best for **Free Performances**
★★★ Curtis Institute of Music, 1726 Locust St. (p 129)

Best **Jazz Club**
★★ Ortlieb's Jazzhaus, 847 N. 3rd St. (p 130)

Best **Rock Club**
★ Johnny Brenda's, 1201 Frankford Ave. (p 130)

Best for **Broadway Productions**
★ The Forrest, 1114 Walnut St. (p 125)

Best for **Outdoor Concerts**
★ Susquehanna Bank Center, 1 Harbour Blvd., Camden (p 130)

Best for **Drama with an Edge**
★ Wilma Theater, 265 S. Broad St. (p 129)

Best for **Cabaret**
★ L'Etage, 624 S. 6th St. (p 132)

Best for **Laid-Back Original Music**
★ Tin Angel, 20 S. 2nd St. (p 131)

Best for **Family Concerts**
★★ World Café Live, 3025 Walnut St. (p 131)

The Kimmel Center for the Performing Arts is home to the Philadelphia Orchestra. Previous page: The Philadelphia Opera Company performs at the Academy of Music in Midtown.

Arts & Entertainment in
Northern Liberties

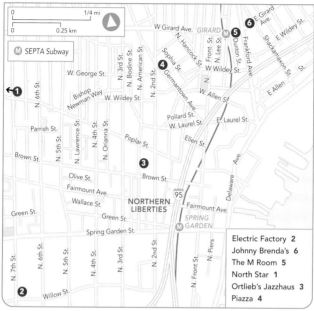

SEPTA Subway

Electric Factory **2**
Johnny Brenda's **6**
The M Room **5**
North Star **1**
Ortlieb's Jazzhaus **3**
Piazza **4**

Arts & Entertainment A to Z

Theater
★★ kids Arden Theatre Company OLD CITY
Two intimate, contemporary performance spaces offer five popular productions each season—adaptations, premieres, and masterpieces—plus two excellent plays for families. *40 N. 2nd St. (btw. Market & Arch sts.).* ☎ *215/922-1122. www.ardentheatre.org. Tickets $30–$48 Bus: 5, 17, 21, 33, 42, 48, 57. Subway: 2nd St. Map p 126.*

★ The Forrest WASHINGTON
WEST   Best for big musicals (*Phantom of the Opera, Jersey Boys*), this spectacular venue was built for $2

million in 1927, when Gilbert & Sullivan launched productions here. *1114 Walnut St. (btw. 11th & 12th sts.).* ☎ *800/447-7400. www.forrest-theatre.com. Tickets $30–$90. Bus: 9, 12, 21, 23, 42. Map p 126.*

Merriam Theater CENTER
CITY   This turn-of-the-20th-century Avenue of the Arts stunner welcomes top Broadway musicals as well as musical and other performances by everyone from Paul Simon to David Sedaris. *250 S. Broad St. (btw. Spruce & Locust sts.).* ☎ *215/893-1999. www.kimmelcenter.org. Tickets $20–$150. Bus: C,*

Arts & Entertainment in
Center City

Academy of Music **12**
Academy of Vocal Arts **7**
Annenberg Center at the
  University of Pennsylvania **5**
Arden Theatre Company **23**
Chris' Jazz Café **11**
Curtis Institute of Music **8**
The Forrest **17**
Helium Comedy Club **4**
Kimmel Center for the
  Performing Arts **15**
L'Etage **21**
Mann Music Center **1**
Merriam Theater **13**
Painted Bride Art Center **22**

Philadelphia Shakespeare
  Theatre **3**
Plays & Players Theater **9**
Prince Music Theater **10**
Society Hill Playhouse **20**
Susquehanna Bank Center **26**
Suzanne Roberts Theatre **16**
The Khyber **25**
Theater of Living Arts **27**
Tin Angel **24**
Tower Theatre **2**
Trocadero **18**
Walnut Street Theater **19**
Wilma Theater **14**
World Café Live **6**

Willow St.

676

N. 10th St.

1/4 mi

0.25 km

Wood St.

Vine St.

New St.

95

22

Vine St.

Franklin Square

N. 5th St.

676

Florist St.

Spring St.

CHINATOWN

Race St.

M

Race St.

Quarry St.

N. 7th St.

CHINATOWN

Cherry St.

National Constitution Center

Cherry St.

Betsy Ross House

N. 10th St.

N. 9th St.

US Mint

N. 3rd St.

N. Front St.

N. Water St.

18

Cuthbert St.

Filbert St.

Independence National Historical Park

Arch St.

☆

OLD CITY

23

Filbert St.

N. 8th St.

N. 7th St.

Independence Visitor Center

5TH

✝ Church St.

Market East Station

M

11TH

8TH

M P 8TH

M

Market St.

M 2ND

S. 11th St.

S. 10th St.

✉

Ranstead St.

S. 7th St.

Liberty Bell Center

The Bourse

S. 3rd St.

S. Bank St.

24

Lettia St.

S. Front St.

25

Chestnut St.

Sansom St.

JEWELERS ROW

Ionic St.

Independence Hall

S. 2nd St.

Ionic St.

26 →

WASHINGTON SQUARE WEST

19

Walnut St.

17

S. 8th St.

Washington Square

Locust St.

✝

Philip Pl

SOCIETY HILL

Dock St.

Dock St.

Irving St.

P 9TH-10TH

S. Washington Sq

Manning St.

Manning Walk

✝ Locust St.

Spruce St.

S. 4th St.

Spruce St.

Delancey St.

S. 2nd St.

Veterans Memorial Park

Spruce St.

Pennsylvania Hospital

S. 7th St.

S. 6th St.

☆

Cypress St.

Cypress St.

Clinton St.

ANTIQUE ROW

Pine St.

Waverly St.

✝

Addison St.

Lombard St.

95

Seger Park

Starr Garden Rec Center

S. Reese St.

Gaskill St.

Old 2nd St.

South St.

20

SOUTH STREET

Kater St.

S. Leithgow St.

27

South St.

Bainbridge St.

S. Percy St.

S. Mildred St.

21

S. American St.

Bainbridge St.

S. Jessup St.

S. 11th St.

S. Clifton St.

Palumbo Playground

Clymer St.

Clymer St.

Monroe St.

Fitzwater St.

Fitzwater St.

S. 10th St.

S. Delhi St.

S. Percy St.

Fulton St.

S. 7th St.

E. Passyunk Ave.

Fulton St.

S. 5th St.

S. 4th St.

FABRIC ROW

ITALIAN MARKET

BELLA VISTA

Christian St.

Montrose St.

M *SEPTA Subway*

P *PATCO Light Rail*

T *Trolley*

✝ *Church*

☆ *Synagogue*

■ *Point of Interest*

✉ *Post Office*

Kimball St.

Carpenter St.

Kimball St.

League St.

S. 8th St.

Kimball St.

League St.

S. Randolph St.

S. 11th St.

Washington Ave.

The Walnut Street Theater hosts Broadway-style productions.

12, 27, 32. Subway: Walnut-Locust. Map p 126.

★ Philadelphia Shakespeare Theatre
RITTENHOUSE The Bard's best-loved plays, two or three of them per year, played traditionally, cleverly re-imagined, or with an easy-to-understand, educational bent, performed in an intimate setting. *2111 Sansom St. (btw. 21st & 22nd sts.).* ☎ *215/496-9722. www.phillyshakespeare.org. Tickets free–$35. Bus: 7, 9, 12, 21, 42. Map p 126.*

★ Plays & Players Theater
Charmingly rickety, this side-street landmark is home to the century-old amateur troupe of the same name, known for classic drama, works-in-progress, and interactive shows. *1714 Delancey St. (btw. 17th & 18th sts., Spruce & Pine sts.).* ☎ *215/735-0630. www.playsand players.org. Tickets $10–$40. Bus: 2, 40. Map p 126.*

Prince Music Theater
CENTER CITY An old picture palace turned modern venue hosts live bands and comedy, filmed performances of the Royal Opera House and Royal Ballet, cabaret, and old movies. *1412 Chestnut St. (btw. Broad & 15th sts.).* ☎ *215/972-1000. www.prince musictheater.org. Tickets (to live performances) $15–$60. Bus: 9, 21, 38,*

42, 124. Subway: City Hall. Map p 126.

Society Hill Playhouse
SOCIETY HILL The self-described "theater for people who don't like theater" has an upstairs main stage known for its original and popular comedy, and a downstairs "Red Room" for smaller productions. *507 S. 8th St. (btw. Lombard & South sts.).* ☎ *215/923-0210. www.societyhill playhouse.com. Tickets $10–$55. Bus: 40, 47. Map p 126.*

Suzanne Roberts Theatre
CENTER CITY Universal access is the concept behind this newest and most iridescent of Broad Street's performing spaces, home base to both the "all premieres" of the Philadelphia Theatre and Koresh Dance companies. *480 S. Broad St. (at Lombard St.).* ☎ *215/985-1400. www. philadelphiatheatrecompany.com. Tickets to Philadelphia Theatre Co. performances $44–$69. Bus: 4, 27, 32, 40. Subway: Lombard-South. Map p 126.*

★ kids Walnut Street Theater
WASHINGTON WEST The country's oldest playhouse (ca. 1809) hosts locally produced Broadway-style productions (*Grease, Fiddler on the Roof*) and children's shows in its 1,100-seat theater, plus experimental works in its adjoining studio

spaces. *825 Walnut St. (at 9th St.).* ☎ *215/574-3550. www.walnut streettheatre.org. Tickets $10–$95. Bus: 9, 12, 21, 42, 47m, 61, 62. Map p 126.*

★ **Wilma Theater** CENTER CITY For drama buffs: A modern, 300-seat space offering modern works, including premieres by playwrights such as Tom Stoppard. *265 S. Broad St. (at Spruce St.).* ☎ *215/546-7824. www.wilmatheater.org. Tickets $39–$66. Bus: 4, 27, 32. Subway: Walnut-Locust. Map p 126.*

Opera, Ballet, Classical
★★★ **Academy of Music** CENTER CITY   The grandest performance hall in town—from its iconic gaslights to its gilded onstage columns—is home to the Pennsylvania Ballet, Philadelphia Opera Company, visiting performers, and traveling musical theater. *240 S. Broad St. (at Locust St.).* ☎ *215/893-1999. www.kimmelcenter.org. Tickets for ballet $20–$125. Bus: 4, 12, 27, 32. Subway: Walnut-Locust. Map p 126.*

★★ **Academy of Vocal Arts** RITTENHOUSE   One of the world's most exclusive opera schools (only 30 students at a time) makes its home in—and gives marvelously intimate performances from—an ornate old townhouse. *1920 Spruce St. (btw. 19th & 20th sts.).* ☎ *215/735-1685. www.avaopera.org. Tickets $48–$83. Bus: 17. Map p 126.*

★★★ **Curtis Institute of Music** RITTENHOUSE   In a rambling limestone mansion is one of the world's finest music schools (Lang-Lang trained here) offering free student recitals (Oct–May Mon, Wed & Fri 8pm). Curtis students also perform full-scale opera at the Prince Music Theater (see above) and symphony orchestra at the Kimmel Center (see below). *1726 Locust St.*

The Academy of Vocal Arts is one of the world's most exclusive opera schools.

(btw. 17th St. & Rittenhouse Sq.). ☎ *215/893-7902. www.curtis.edu. Tickets free–$40. Bus: 2, 9, 12, 21, 42. Map p 126.*

Music/Performance Halls
★ **Annenberg Center at the University of Pennsylvania** UNIVERSITY CITY   A mixed bag of productions take place at this modern, double-stage space, from local jazz to the International Children's Festival to dance. *3680 Walnut St. (btw. 36th & 38th sts.).* ☎ *215/898-6702. www.pennpresents.org. Tickets $10–$55. Bus: 21. Trolley: 11, 13, 34, 36. Subway: 34th St. Map p 126.*

★★★ **Kimmel Center for the Performing Arts** CENTER CITY   This dramatic glass and steel vault includes a 2,500-seat cello-shaped concert hall built for the Philadelphia Orchestra (but performed in by all manner of musical acts) and a 650-seat space for chamber music, dance, and drama. *300 S. Broad St. (at Spruce St.).* ☎ *215/893-1999. www.kimmelcenter.org. Tickets* for *Philadelphia Orchestra $26–$180. Bus: 4, 12, 27, 32. Subway: Walnut-Locust. Map p 126.*

★★ Mann Music Center FAIR-MOUNT PARK   This summertime amphitheater has covered seating and picnicking on the grass for concerts by Yo-Yo Ma, the Indigo Girls, John Legend, Barenaked Ladies, and more. *5201 Parkside Ave. (at Belmont Ave.).* ☎ *215/546-7900. www.manncenter.org. Tickets $15–$79. Bus: CCLB, 40, 52. Trolley: 10. Map p 126.*

★ Susquehanna Bank Center CAMDEN   Just across the Delaware River, this 25,000-capacity summer amphitheater has had Coldplay, Jimmy Buffett, Dave Matthews, and Megadeath perform al fresco. *1 Harbour Blvd., Camden, NJ.* ☎ *856/365-1300. www.livenation. com. Tickets $25–$110. Bus (to ferry): 25. Map p 126.*

Jazz & Blues Venues
★ Chris' Jazz Café CENTER CITY   Center City's only spot for local jazz, this cozy, casual find has a simple bar menu and a cool vibe. Great for date night. *1421 Sansom St. (btw. Broad & 15th sts.).* ☎ *215/568-3131. www.chrisjazzcafe.com. Cover $5–$20. Bus: 9, 12, 21, 38, 42, 142. Subway: Walnut-Locust. Map p 126.*

★★ Ortlieb's Jazzhaus NORTH-ERN LIBERTIES   Dimly lit, hard to find, this joint gets smokin' when Mickey Roker (Dizzy Gillespie's drummer) heads up the Hausband on Tuesday Jazz Jams. *847 N. 3rd St. (btw. Brown & Poplar sts.).* ☎ *267/324-3348. www.ortliebsjazzhaus.com. Cover $3–$10. Bus: 5, 57. Subway: Spring Garden St. Map p 125.*

★ Painted Bride Art Center OLD CITY   This effervescent, welcoming art gallery doubles as a performance space for

contemporary music, dance, and theater—and Philadelphia's longest-running jazz series. *230 Vine St. (btw. 2nd & 3rd sts.).* ☎ *215/925-9914. www.paintedbride.org. Tickets $20–$25. Bus: 5, 25, 57. Map p 126.*

Popular Concert Venues
Electric Factory NORTHERN LIB-ERTIES   A storied industrial setting for medium-large, all-ages shows by likes of Smash Mouth, Ani DiFranco, Fall Out Boy, Rancid, Mos Def, and Regina Spektor. *421 N. 7th St. (btw. Callowhill & Spring Garden sts.).* ☎ *215/627-1332. www.electric factory.info. Tickets $20–$50. Bus: 43, 47, 47m. Map p 125.*

★ Johnny Brenda's NORTHERN LIBERTIES/FISHTOWN   This dive-bar turned music venue/hipster gastro-pub has an upstairs stage for everything from indie folk groups to death metal acts. *1201 Frankford Ave. (at E. Girard Ave.).* ☎ *215/739-9684. www.johnny brendas.com. Tickets $10–$20. Bus: 5, 25. Trolley: 15. Subway: Girard Ave. Map p 125.*

The Khyber OLD CITY   Philly's oldest taproom—note the carved gargoyles above the bar—puts its small upstairs stage to use with nightly visits from up-and-coming local rock bands and DJs. *56 S. 2nd St. (btw. Market & Chestnut sts.).* ☎ *215/238-5888. www.thekhyber. com. Cover $5–$12. Bus: 5, 17, 21, 42, 48, 121. Subway: 2nd St. Map p 126.*

The M Room NORTHERN LIBER-TIES/FISHTOWN   Original, often experimental music shares the weekly bill with independent films, art openings, and DJs at the out-of-the-way M Room. *15 W. Girard Ave. (btw. Front St. & Frankford Ave.).* ☎ *215/739-5577. www.mroomphilly. com. Cover $7–$10. Bus: 5, 25.*

Ortlieb's Jazzhaus hosts some serious jazz musicians such as Mickey Roker.

Trolley: 15. Subway: Girard Ave. Map p 125.

North Star FAIRMOUNT   On a neighborhood's edge, this mid-size venue specializes in rock, from tons of local acts to the White Stripes to Dick Dale. There are pool tables and finger foods, too. *2629 Poplar St. (at 27th St.).* ☎ *215/787-0488. www.northstarbar.com. Tickets $5–$35. Bus: 32, 48. Map p 125.*

Piazza NORTHERN LIBERTIES World music festivals, DJ'd dance parties (plus family movies and Phillies games on the big screen) are part of the scene at this al fresco courtyard of shops, bars, and condos. *2nd St. & Germantown Ave. (at Hancock St.).215/825-7552. www. atthepiazza.com. Free admission. Bus: 5, 25. Trolley: 15. Subway: Girard Ave. Map p 125.*

★ **Theater of Living Arts** SOUTH STREET   Funk bands, French hip-hop acts, vintage Brit rockers, and all-American comedians fill the marquee of the TLA, a bare-bones, standing-room-only venue where big-time local acts like The Roots sell out fast. *334 South St. (btw. 3rd & 4th sts.).* ☎ *215/922-1011. www.tlaphilly.com. Tickets $5–$35. Bus: 40, 57. Map p 126.*

★ **Tin Angel** OLD CITY   Singer-songwriters are the bread and butter of this subdued upstairs space, starring folks such as Dar Williams, Ritchie Havens, Everything But The Girl, and Jeffrey Gaines. There's an international restaurant downstairs, too. *20 S. 2nd St. (btw. Market & Chestnut sts.).* ☎ *215/928-0978. www.tinangel.com. Tickets $10–$25. Bus: 5, 17, 21, 33, 42, 48. Subway: 2nd St. Map p 126.*

★ **Tower Theatre** WEST PHILLY/ UPPER DARBY   All post-Depression-era gilt and scrollwork, this shabby-majestic, 3,500-seat venue is a great spot to catch anyone from Weird Al to Joe Satriani. *19 S. 69th St. (at Ludlow St. off Market St.).* ☎ *610/352-2887. www.the towerphilly.com. Tickets $35–$65. Subway: 69th St. Map p 126.*

★ **Trocadero** CHINATOWN Goth acts, punk bands, The Dandy Warhols, and 2 Live Crew have all performed beneath the timeworn vaulted ceilings of this 1870s vaudeville house. *1003 Arch St. (btw. 10th & 11th sts.).* ☎ *215/922-6888. www.thetroc.com. Tickets $10–$32. Bus: 23, 48, 61. Map p 126.*

★★ **kids** **World Café Live** UNIVERSITY CITY   Operated by Penn's indie music radio station, this

Rock bands play nightly at The Khyber.

multi-tasking venue offers a cafe stage and a two-level, 1,000-capacity space for concerts by They Might be Giants, Nick Lowe, Zap Mama, and kids' acts. *3025 Walnut St. (btw. 30th & 31st sts.).* ☎ *215/222-1400. www.worldcafelive.com. Tickets $8–$50. Bus: 21, 42. Train: 30th St. Map p 126.*

Cabaret

★ **L'Etage** SOUTH STREET
Upstairs from a creperie (p 102), this red-curtained lounge-with-a-dance-floor offers a mixed bag of evening pleasures, from weekday poetry slams, comedy, and cabaret to weekend DJs. *624 S. 6th St. (at Bainbridge St.).* ☎ *215/592-0656. www.creperie-beaumonde.com. Cover free–$15. Bus: 40, 47. Map p 126.*

Comedy

★ **Helium Comedy Club** RITTENHOUSE   Knowns (John Oliver, Rich Vos, and Kevin Pollack) and not-yet-knowns (Tues is open-mic night) take the stage in front of a friendly, small, table-sat crowd. *2031 Sansom St. (btw. 20th & 21st sts.).* ☎ *215/496-9001. www.helium-comedy.com. Tickets $5–$40. Bus: 9, 12, 17, 21, 42. Map p 126.* ●

Scoring Tickets

For week-of discounts, plus an up-to-date list of theatrical and artistic goings-on, visit the Greater Philadelphia Cultural Alliance's website at www.phillyfunguide.com, or call ☎ **215/557-7811.** Tickets to the Philadelphia Orchestra, Pennsylvania Ballet, Academy of Music, and Merriam and Forrest Theaters can be had via Ticket Philadelphia (☎ **215/893-1999;** www.ticketphiladelphia. org), or purchased directly from the Kimmel Center's box office open daily until 6pm, later on performance nights (see p 129). A lucky few can score a single $10 "community rush" ticket at 5:30pm the night of an evening performance or 11:30am for a matinee.

The Best Hotels

Hotel Best Bets

Best at the **Airport**
★ Aloft $–$$ *4301 Island Ave.* (p 137)

Best for **Kids**
★ Sheraton Society Hill $$–$$$ *1 Dock St.* (p 141)

Best for **Pets**
★ Loews Philadelphia Hotel $$ *1200 Market St.* (p 140)

Best for **Beds**
★★ Westin Philadelphia $$–$$$ *99 S. 17th St.* (p 142)

Best for a **Splurge**
★★★ Four Seasons $$$–$$$$ *1 Logan Square* (p 138)

Best for **Views**
★ Hyatt Regency at Penn's Landing $$–$$$ *201 S. Columbus Blvd.* (p 139)

Best **Gym**
★★ Hyatt at the Bellevue $$–$$$ *1415 Chancellor Ct.* (p 139)

Best for a **Long-Term Stay**
★★ AKA Rittenhouse Square $$–$$$$$ *135 S. 18th St.* (p 137)

Best Near the **Convention Center**
★★ Four Points by Sheraton $$–$$$ *1201 Race St.* (p 138)

Best for **Celeb Spotting**
★★★ Rittenhouse Hotel $$$–$$$$ *210 W. Rittenhouse Square* (p 141)

Best for **Glamour**
★★★ Ritz-Carlton Philadelphia $$$–$$$$$ *10 S. Broad St.* (p 141)

Best for **Couples**
★★ Penn's View Hotel $$–$$$ *Front & Market sts.* (p 140)

Best **Historic Lodging**
★★★ Thomas Bond House $$ *129 S. 2nd St.* (p 142)

Best for **Bargain Rooms**
★ Alexander Inn $$ *301 S. 12th St.* (p 137)

Best **Bed & Breakfast**
★★ La Reserve B&B $–$$ *1804–1806 Pine St.* (p 139)

The boutique Morris House Hotel is located inside a former historic home. Previous page: The Rittenhouse Hotel is an excellent place to spot celebs.

East of Broad Lodging

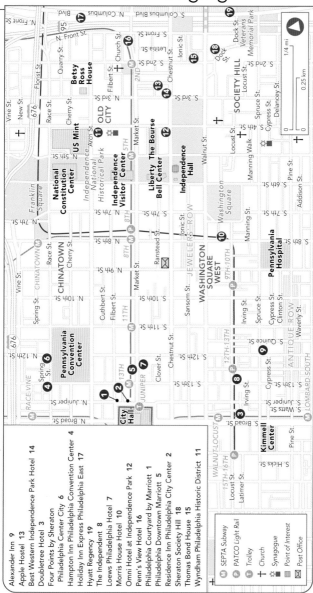

Alexander Inn 9
Apple Hostel 13
Best Western Independence Park Hotel 14
Doubletree Hotel 3
Four Points by Sheraton
    Philadelphia Center City 6
Hampton Inn Philadelphia Convention Center 4
Holiday Inn Express Philadelphia East 17
Hyatt Regency 19
The Independent 8
Loews Philadelphia Hotel 7
Morris House Hotel 10
Omni Hotel at Independence Park 12
Penn's View Hotel 16
Philadelphia Courtyard by Marriott 1
Philadelphia Downtown Marriott 5
Residence Inn Philadelphia City Center 2
Sheraton Society Hill 18
Thomas Bond House 15
Wyndham Philadelphia Historic District 11

SEPTA Subway
PATCO Light Rail
Trolley
Church
Synagogue
Point of Interest
Post Office

West of Broad Lodging

- Ⓜ SEPTA Subway
- Ⓟ PATCO Light Rail
- Ⓣ Trolley
- † Church

Hotels A to Z

★★ AKA Rittenhouse Square
RITTENHOUSE SQUARE Chic, just like its address, this all-suites spot is popular among discerning business travelers for week-long stays (although stays as brief as 2 nights are available). *135 S. 18th St. (btw. Walnut & Sansom sts.).* ☎ *888/252-0180 or 215/825-7000. www.stayaka.com. 78 units. Suites $195–$415. AE, DISC, MC, V. Bus: 9, 12, 21, 42. Map p 136.*

★ Alexander Inn WASHINGTON
WEST Simple little rooms—ask for a corner room; they're bigger—help make this boutique gayborhood spot affordable and popular. *301 S. 12th St. (at Spruce St.).* ☎ *877/253-9466 or 215/923-3535. www.alexanderinn.com. 48 units. Doubles from $129–$169 w/breakfast. AE, DC, DISC, MC, V. Bus: 23. Map p 135.*

★ Aloft Philadelphia AIRPORT
A modern, lower-priced, fast-paced version of the glitzy W, with platform beds, Wi-Fi, and a 24-hour snack bar. *4301 Island Ave. (near I-95).* ☎ *877/462-5638 or 267/298-1700. www.starwoodhotels.com. 136 units. Doubles $98–$179. AE, DC, MC, V. Bus: 68. Train: Airport Line. Map p 136.*

Apple Hostel OLD CITY Dorm-
style bunking, a TV lounge with billiards, shared baths, free pasta dinners (Wed), and pub crawls with strangers—this place is like college, only cheaper. *32 S. Bank St. (btw. 2nd & 3rd sts., Market & Chestnut sts.).* ☎ *877/275-1971 or 215/922-0222. www.applehostels.com. 70 beds. Dorm $35–$37; private/semi-private room $73–$87. MC, V. Bus: 17, 21, 33, 42, 48, 57. Subway: 2nd St. Map p 135.*

The modern Aloft Philadelphia is a stylish alternative near the airport.

Best Western Independence Park Hotel
OLD CITY A circa-1856 dry-goods store offers high-ceilinged quarters just 2 blocks from Independence Hall. *235 Chestnut St. (btw. 2nd & 3rd sts.).* ☎ *800/624-2988 or 215/922-4443. www.independenceparkhotel.com. 36 units. Doubles $163–$330 w/breakfast. AE, DC, DISC, MC, V. Bus: 17, 21, 33, 42, 48, 57. Subway: 2nd St. Map p 135.*

★ Club Quarters Philadelphia
RITTENHOUSE This handsome, business-savvy boutique chain also makes its sleek, modern, cozy rooms—many with kitchenette—available to non-members. *1628 Chestnut St. (at 17th St.).* ☎ *215/282-5000. www.clubquarters.com. Doubles $119–$249. AE, DC, DISC, MC, V. Bus: 2, 9, 21, 42. Map p 136.*

Doubletree Hotel CENTER
CITY Location, location, location (and warm chocolate chip cookies):

The Four Seasons Hotel has an outstanding lounge area.

This business traveler's default has views to the Delaware River from higher floors. *237 S. Broad St. (at Locust St.).* ☎ *800/222-8733 or 215/893-1600. www.doubletree hotels.com. 427 units. Doubles $89–$234. AE, DC, DISC, MC, V. Bus: 4, 12, 27, 32. Subway: Walnut-Locust. Map p 135.*

★ Embassy Suites Center City

LOGAN CIRCLE   A cylindrical 1960s apartment building that's been converted to an all-suites hotel with balconies; nice for a longer stay. *1776 Ben Franklin Pkwy. (at 18th St.).* ☎ *800/362-2779 or 215/ 561-1776. www.embassysuites.hilton. com. 288 units. Suites $136–$296 w/ breakfast. AE, DC, DISC, MC, V. Bus: 2, 32, 33. Map p 136.*

★★ Four Points by Sheraton Philadelphia Center City

CONVENTION CENTER   The vibe, the bar, and the tiny rooms of a Manhattan boutique hotel; across the street from the Reading Terminal Market. *1201 Race St. (at 12th St.).* ☎ *215/496-2700. www.fourpoints philadelphiacitycenter.com. 92 units. Doubles $169–$219. AE, DC, MC, V. Bus: 23, 61. Map p 135.*

★★★ Four Seasons Hotel

LOGAN CIRCLE   Top-notch service is the hallmark of this elegant and understated award winner, with a marvelous restaurant, lounge, and spa. *1 Logan Square (at 18th St. & Ben Franklin Pkwy.).* ☎ *800/332-3442 or 215/963-1500. www.four seasons.com. 364 units. Doubles $299–$389. AE, DC, MC, V. Bus: 2, 32, 33, 48. Map p 136.*

Hampton Inn Philadelphia Convention Center

CENTER CITY   This reliable chain offers straightforward lodging, friendly service, and an indoor pool. *1301 Race St. (at 13th St.).* ☎ *800/ 426-7866 or 215/665-9100. www. hamptoninn.com. 250 units. Doubles $139–$199 w/breakfast. AE, DC, DISC, MC, V. Bus: 2, 16, 23, 27. Subway: Race Vine. Map p 135.*

Holiday Inn Express Philadelphia E

PENN'S LANDING   Students and seniors frequent this basic spot, a bit isolated from Old City but with great river views. *100 N. Columbus Blvd. (near the Ben Franklin Bridge.).* ☎ *800/465-4329 or 215/627-7900. www.ihg.com. 184 units. Doubles from $119. AE, DC, DISC, MC, V. Bus: 25. Map p 135.*

★★ Hotel Palomar

RITTENHOUSE   Old Art Deco offices, now cozily contemporary and eco-minded, make up this boutique hotel from Kimpton. Most rooms have laptops. Many have great city views. *117 S. 17th St. (at Sansom St.).* ☎ *888/725-1778 or 215/563-5006. www.kimptonhotels.com. 247 units. Doubles $169–$469. AE, DISC, MC, V. Bus: 2, 9, 12, 21, 42. Map p 136.*

★★ Hyatt at the Bellevue

BROAD STREET   Once the country's most opulent hotel (in 1904), this Hyatt keeps up-to-date with spacious rooms, goose-down duvets, and a great gym. *200 South Broad St. (btw. Walnut & Locust sts.).* ☎ *800/223-1234 or 215/893-1234. www.parkphiladelphia.hyatt.com. 172 units. Doubles $179–$259. AE, DC, DISC, MC, V. Bus: 4, 9, 12, 21, 27, 32, 42. Subway: Walnut-Locust. Map p 136.*

★ kids Hyatt Regency PENN'S

LANDING   Your only waterfront option, this Art Deco–style complex boasts an indoor pool overlooking docked old ships and plenty of space for spreading out. *201 S. Columbus Blvd. (at Dock St.)* ☎ *800/233-1234 or 215/928-1234. www.pennslanding.hyatt.com. 348 units. Doubles $149–$220. AE, DC, MC, V. Bus: 25. Map p 135.*

★ The Independent CENTER

CITY   This Georgian Revival building has contemporary appointments, fireplaces in some rooms, and cathedral ceilings in others. It's in the heart of the gayborhood, near a somewhat shady-dealings corner. *1234 Locust St. (btw. 12th & 13th sts.).* ☎ *215/772-1440. www. theindependenthotel.com. 24 units. Doubles $159–$279. AE, MC, V. Bus: 9, 12, 21, 23, 42. Subway: Walnut-Locust. Map p 135.*

★★ La Reserve B&B RITTEN-

HOUSE   An elegant B&B in a pair of 1850s townhouses. Half the rooms are studios or suites for not much more than a double. Weekends, the Continental breakfast gives way to home-cooked. *1804–1806 Pine St. (btw. 18th & 19th sts.).* ☎ *888/405-8567 or 215/735-1137. www.lareservebandb.com. 12 units. Doubles $80–$155 w/breakfast. AE, DISC, MC, V. Bus: 2, 17, 40. Map p 136.*

★ The Latham RITTENHOUSE

A landmark hotel in the first half of the 20th century, this now-contemporary hotel brings to mind an efficiently run European hostelry. *135*

The Hyatt at the Bellevue was once the country's most opulent hotel.

S. 17th St. (at Walnut St.). ☎ 877/528-4261 or 215/563-7474. www.lathamhotel.com. 139 units. Doubles $80–$155. AE, DC, DISC, MC, V. Bus: 2, 9, 12, 21, 42. Map p 136.

★ kids Loews Philadelphia Hotel

CENTER CITY This hotel is beloved by aesthetes for its international style and Cartier wall clocks, and adored by swimmers for its lap pool with a view and children (and traveling pets) for its toy cache. Rooms tend to be small. 1200 Market St. (at 12th St.). ☎ 800/235-6397 or 215/627-1200. www.loewshotels.com. 581 units. Doubles $159–$199. AE, DC, DISC, MC, V. Bus: 17, 23, 33, 38, 44, 48, 62. Subway: 13th St. Map p 135.

★★ Morris House Hotel

WASHINGTON SQUARE Antique portrait paintings, uneven floorboards, and afternoon tea add to the charm of this 1787 house turned boutique hotel. Request a courtyard room to avoid street noise. 225 S. 8th St. (btw. Walnut & Locust sts.). ☎ 215/922-2446. www.morrishousehotel.com. 15 units. Doubles $139–$189 w/breakfast. AE, MC, V. Bus: 9, 12, 21, 42, 47, 61, 62. Map p 135.

★ Omni Hotel at Independence Park

OLD CITY A primo location for history buffs, this polished, pastel spot is across the street from Independence Park and has a staff known for its knowledge of the district. 401 Chestnut St. (at 4th St.). ☎ 800/843-6664 or 215/925-0000. www.omnihotels.com. 150 units. Doubles $189–$309. AE, DC, DISC, MC, V. Bus: 9, 21, 42, 57. Subway: 5th St. Map p 135.

★★ Penn's View Hotel

OLD CITY This hidden gem has European, family-run appeal—and a fantastic wine bar (See p 122). Front & Market sts. ☎ 800/331-7634 or 215/922-7600. www.pennsviewhotel.com. 51 units. Doubles $139–$259 w/breakfast. AE, MC, V. Bus: 5, 17, 21, 42, 48. Subway: 2nd St. Map p 135.

★ Philadelphia Airport Marriott

AIRPORT If you're stuck at the airport and have just a few hours to sleep, this is the quiet, connected place to do it. 1 Arrivals Rd., Terminal B (via skywalk to PHL Airport). ☎ 800/682-4087 or 215/492-9000. www.marriott.com. 419 units. Doubles $139–$329. AE, DC, DISC, MC, V. Bus: 37, 108, 115. Train: R1. Map p 136.

★★ Philadelphia Courtyard by Marriott

CENTER CITY This is my favorite of the trio of Convention Center-ed Marriotts because of its circa-1926 setting and City Hall view. 21 N. Juniper St. (at Broad & Filbert sts.). ☎ 888/887-8130 or 215/496-3200. www.marriott.com. 498 units. Doubles $103–$319. AE, DC, DISC, MC, V. Bus: 27, 31, 32, 124, 125. Trolley: 10, 11, 13, 43, 36. Subway: City Hall or 13th St. Map p 135.

Philadelphia Marriott Downtown

CENTER CITY The biggest in town, this high-tech hotel is attached via skyway to the Pennsylvania Convention Center. It often books to capacity with business folk. 1201 Market St. (btw. 12th & 13th sts.). ☎ 800/320-5744 or 215/625-2900. www.marriott.com. 1,408 units. Doubles $109–$389. AE, DC, MC, V. Bus: 17, 23, 33, 38, 44, 48, 62. Subway: 13th St. Map p 135.

★ Radisson Blu—Warwick Hotel

RITTENHOUSE In 2013, this history-touched half-condo, half-hotel was converted into a sleek, contemporary member of Radisson's Blu brand. 220 S. 17th St. (at Locust St.). ☎ 800/967-9033 or 215/735-6000. www.radisson.com. 301 units. Doubles $155–$389. AE,

DC, DISC, MC, V. Bus: 2, 9, 12, 21, 42. Map p 136.

Residence Inn Philadelphia Center City CENTER CITY This

suites-only spot is surprisingly quiet, considering its location as the single most central hotel in town. City Hall views and a high-tech fitness center. *1 E. Penn Sq. (at Broad & Market sts.).* ☎ *800/331-3131 or 215/557-0005. www.marriott. com. 269 units. Suites $169–$339 w/ breakfast. AE, DC, MC, V. Bus: 27, 31, 32, 124, 125. Trolley: 10, 11, 13, 43, 36. Subway: City Hall or 13th St. Map p 135.*

★★ Rittenhouse 1715 RITTEN-

HOUSE In a city mansion on a leafy little street just off the south-east corner of upmarket Rittenhouse Square, this traditional, boutique-y spot has a European vibe. *1715 Rit-tenhouse Square St. (btw. 17th & 18th sts.).* ☎ *877/791-6500 or 215/546-6500. www.rittenhouse1715.com. 23 units. Doubles $160–$345 w/ breakfast. AE, DC, MC, V. Bus: 2, 12, 21, 42. Map p 136.*

★★★ kids Rittenhouse Hotel

RITTENHOUSE This elegant, modern hotel has a restaurant over-looking the treetops of Rittenhouse Square, an amazing gym, salon, and spa. Jack Nicholson stays here when he's in town. *210 W. Ritten-house Square (btw. Locust & Walnut sts.).* ☎ *800/635-1042 or 215/546-9000. www.rittenhousehotel.com. 98 units. Doubles $224–$349. AE, DC, MC, V. Bus: 9, 12, 17, 21, 42. Map p 136.*

★★★ The Ritz-Carlton Phila-delphia CENTER CITY This all-

marble former bank has butlered bath service and a lounge in the formidable colonnaded lobby. It's very posh. *10 S. Broad St. (btw. City Hall & Chestnut St.).* ☎ *800/241-3333 or 215/523-8000. www.ritz carlton.com. 299 units. Doubles $249–$519. AE, DC, DISC, MC, V. Bus: 4, 9, 16, 21, 27, 31, 32, 38, 42, 124. Subway: City Hall. Map p 136.*

Sheraton Philadelphia Down-town LOGAN CIRCLE As big as

a city block, this cement behemoth feels like a cross between a conven-tion center and a cruise ship. *1201 N. 7th St. (at Race St.)* ☎ *800/ 325-3535 or 215/448-2000. www. sheraton.com. 757 units. Doubles $149–$249. AE, DC, MC, V. Bus: 2, 27. Map p 136.*

★ kids Sheraton Society Hill

OLD CITY On a curvy cobble-stone street, this low, sprawling brick building offers traditional rooms, a lush atrium, and a splashy

The posh Ritz-Carlton Philadelphia.

indoor pool. *1 Dock St. (at 2nd & Walnut sts.).* ☎ *800/325-3535 or 215/238-6000. www.sheraton.com/ societyhill. 364 units. Doubles $169–$269. AE, DC, MC, V. Bus: 21, 42. Map p 135.*

★★ Sofitel Philadelphia RITTENHOUSE

Low-key luxury, a "bonjour" at the door, and fresh croissants at breakfast; this French hotel is close to the city's poshest shopping and dining. *120 S. 17th St. (at Sansom St.).* ☎ *800/763-4835 or 215/569-8300. www.sofitel.com. 306 units. Doubles $144–$285. AE, DC, MC, V. Bus: 2, 9, 12, 21, 42. Map p 136.*

Sonesta Philadelphia RITTENHOUSE

Airline pilots and conventioneers come for the large rooms and easy city access in a nonsense-free setting. *1800 Market St. (at 18th St.).* ☎ *215/561-7500. www.sonesta. com. 445 units. Doubles $180–$220. AE, DC, MC, V. Bus: 17, 31, 32, 33, 38, 44, 48, 62, 124, 125. Trolley: 10, 11, 13, 34, 26. Subway: 15th St. Map p 136.*

★★★ Thomas Bond House

OLD CITY Named for its first occupant, Thomas Bond (1712–1784 and co-founder of Pennsylvania Hospital), this cheerful, colonial B&B is as historic as a Philly overnight gets. *129 S. 2nd St. (btw. Chestnut & Samson sts.).* ☎ *800/ 845-2663 or 215/923-8504. www. thomasbondhousebandb.com. 12 units. Doubles $125–$190 w/breakfast. AE, DISC, MC, V. Bus: 21, 42. Subway: 2nd St. Map p 135.*

★★ Westin Philadelphia RITTENHOUSE

Handsomely clubby atmosphere—with the best beds in town—is tucked into one of Philadelphia's iconic skyscrapers. *99 S. 17th St. (btw. Market & Chestnut sts.).* ☎ *800/228-3000 or 215/563-1600. www.westinphiladelphiahotel. com. 294 units. Doubles $159–$299.*

The historic Thomas Bond House is a cheerful B&B.

AE, DISC, MC, V. Bus: 2, 9, 21, 42. Subway: 15th St. Map p 136.

kids Windsor Suites Philadelphia LOGAN CIRCLE

Great for families whose kids don't mind sleeping on a pullout sofa, this bargain-priced, all-suites offering isn't super fancy, but it's really close to the museums. *1700 Benjamin Franklin Pkwy. (at 17th St.).* ☎ *877/784-8379 or 215/981-5678. www.the windsorsuites.com. Suites from $149–$249. AE, DC, DISC, MC, V. Bus: 2, 32, 33, 48. Map p 136.*

Wyndham Philadelphia Historic District OLD CITY

Nothing fancy: Just an easy-to-access, eight-floor hotel with nice rooms that's convenient to historical sites, galleries, and shopping. There's a rooftop pool, too. *400 Arch St. (at 4th St.).* ☎ *215/923-8660. www. wyndham.com. 364 units. Doubles $127–$199. AE, DC, DISC, MC, V. Bus: 5, 44, 57. Map p 135.* ●

10 The Best Day Trips & Excursions

The Best Day Trips & Excursions

The Best of Brandywine Valley

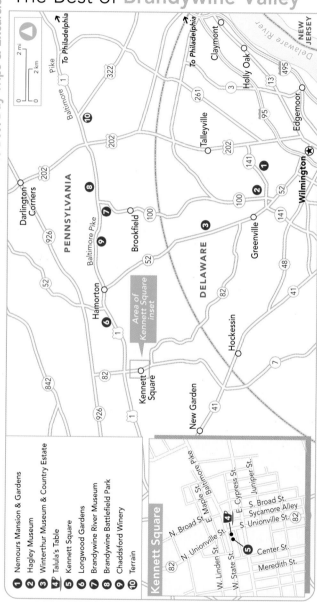

❶ Nemours Mansion & Gardens
❷ Hagley Museum
❸ Winterthur Museum & Country Estate
❹ Talula's Table
❺ Kennett Square
❻ Longwood Gardens
❼ Brandywine River Museum
❽ Brandywine Battlefield Park
❾ Chaddsford Winery
❿ Terrain

Previous page: An Amish horse-and-buggy travels through Lancaster County.

The bucolic, historic countryside around the Brandywine River in Delaware has largely been defined by its two most famous families: First came the entrepreneurial, elegant, and munificent du Ponts. Next, the earthy, cerebral, prolific, and certainly artistic Wyeths. See this region, and you'll see them, and then some. *Tip:* Get the Brandywine Treasure Trail Passport (www.visit wilmingtonde.com) for admission to 11 top area attractions, including all of those mentioned below, for $35 (May 25–Sept 2 only). START: **I-95 S for about 23 miles to Wilmington, then 82 to Kennett Sq., then Baltimore Pike (Rt. 1) to Longwood & Chadds Ford; the drive takes approx. 1 hr.**

❶ Nemours Mansion & Gardens. To experience the opulence of Alfred I. du Pont's circa-1910, Louis XVI-style chateau and Petit-Trianon–modeled garden, with its 23-karat gold statuary, reserve the required tour well in advance. It takes 3 hours, so it's not for everyone. ⏱ 3 hrs. *1600 Rockland Rd., Wilmington, DE.* ☎ *302/651-6912. www.nemoursmansion.org. Tours $15 (ages 12 and up only). May–Dec, Tues–Sat at 9:30am, noon, & 3pm; Sun at noon & 3pm.*

❷ ★★ Hagley Museum. More du Pont acreage offering a covered Georgian manse and gardens, industrial workmen's community, and an interactive science exhibit highlighting DuPont materials (try on a space suit; sit in Jeff Gordon's NASCAR racer). ⏱ *1 hr. Rte. 141 (200 Hagley Rd.), Wilmington, DE.* ☎ *302/658-2400. www.hagley.org. Admission $14 adults, $10 seniors & students, $5 children 6–14. Daily 9:30am–4:30pm.*

❸ ★★★ kids Winterthur Museum & Country Estate. The best of the du Pont estates has the country's foremost collection of American decorative arts, including gems of interior architecture from every Eastern seaboard colony, carefully removed and reassembled here: a Montmorenci stair hall, Shaker rooms, and a grand dining hall. In spring, extensive gardens bloom with azaleas. Kids can explore a 3-acre "enchanted woods." Weather permitting, tram tours are offered March to

Winterthur Museum & Country Estate has America's foremost collection of decorative arts.

Christmas. Christmastime is busiest, with splendid holiday trimmings. The gift shops are fabulous. ⏱ *1 hr. Rte. 52., Winterthur, DE* ☎ *800/448-3883. www.winterthur.org. Admission $18 adults, $16 seniors & students, $5 children 2–11. Tues–Sun 10am–5pm.*

4 ★★★ **Talula's Table.** This charming country market sells artisan cheeses, homemade soups, petite sandwiches, awesome fruit tarts, and coffee. (Come for lunch; scoring the sole dinner table is next to impossible.) *102 W. State St.* ☎ *610/444-8255. www.talulastable.com. $–$$.*

5 ★★ **Kennett Square.** First inhabited by the Lenape Native American tribe, this village became a stopover during the Revolutionary War, then home to free Quakers who established safe havens along the Underground Railroad. A short walk around the historic borough—from State Street to Union, then Mulberry, then back up Broad Street—reveals Queen Anne, Gothic Revival, Italianate, and Tudor architecture. There are plenty of shops. If you dine here, order anything with mushrooms; Kennett Square is the "mushroom capital of the world." Local farmers produce more than 400 million delicious pounds of fungi each year. ⏱ *1 hr. Historic Kennett Square Visitors Center, 106 W. State St., Kennett Square, PA.* ☎ *610/444-8188. www.historic kennettsquare.com.*

6 ★★★ **kids Longwood Gardens.** One of the world's greatest gardens owes its existence to Pierre S.—you guessed it—du Pont, who devoted his life to horticulture and turned a 19th century arboretum into the ultimate 1,077-acre green estate with its own visitor center to get you oriented. Among the must-see attractions: The main garden fountain puts on water shows June to September (daily at noon, 2, and 4pm, plus half-hour illuminated shows Fri–Sat evenings). A topiary garden surrounds a 37-foot sundial. Ponds are filled with massive lily pads. Four acres of bronze and glass conservatories include the Orangery, practically overflowing with African violets, century-old bonsai trees, tropicals, seasonal plants, and visiting collections—they're just a sampling of Longwood's holdings. Almost everywhere, the "no-touching" rule applies, except in a 3,000-square-foot children's garden, with 17 splash fountains, two mazes, a grotto, and umpteen kid-friendly plants. Du Pont's lovely country residence offers a "heritage" collection that includes 2,000-year-old Native

The estate at Longwood Gardens is more than 1,000 acres.

The Brandywine River Museum displays art from the Wyeth family collection.

American spear points. Although springtime is a pleasant time to visit, winter holidays are marvelous, too, with strolling carolers, pipe organ and ice-skating performances, and (naturally) decorated trees galore. ⏱ 1½ hrs. 1001 Longwood Rd. (at Rte. 1), Kennett Square. ☎ 800/737-5500 or 610/388-1000. www.long woodgardens.org. Admission $18 adults, $15 seniors, $8 students, free for children 4 & under. Daily 9am–6pm (open to 10pm daily Nov 28–Jan 12 and Fri–Sat Apr–Sept).

❼ ★★ Brandywine River Museum. Art by three generations of Wyeths—N.C., Carolyn, Andrew, and Jamie, all locals—is on display at this 19th-century gristmill. (If you're lucky, you can see this work via Victoria Wyeth, Andrew's granddaughter, who leads tours Mon–Sat at 2 and 3pm.) The museum—which also contains illustrations and landscape paintings by other American artists—also offers off-site tours (via shuttle bus and for an additional $8) of N.C.'s house and studio, and the Kuerner Farm ($8), where Andrew found so much inspiration. ⏱ 1 hr. Rte. 1 & Rte. 100, Chadds Ford. ☎ 610/388-2700. www.brandywine museum.org. Admission $12 adults, $8 seniors & students, free for children 5 & under. Daily 9:30am–4:30pm.

❽ ★ Brandywine Battlefield Park. Great for a hike, this site hosted a rare full-army clash between Continental and British troops in September 1777 and has a replica of Washington and Lafayette's headquarters. ⏱ ½ hr. 1491 Baltimore Pike (Rte. 1), Chadds Ford. ☎ 610/459-3342. www.brandywine battlefield.org. Free admission to grounds; house $8 adults, $7 seniors, $5 children 6–17. May–Dec 23 Tues–Sat 9am–4pm, Sun noon–4pm; Apr Thurs–Sat 9am–4pm, Sun noon–4pm; Mar 10–31 Fri–Sat 9am–4pm, Sun noon–4pm.

❾ Chaddsford Winery. This 17th-century barn, surrounded by 300 mineral-rich acres, is the closest Pennsylvania gets to Napa. The friendly vintners offer free tastings and cellar tours, allow picnicking, and host al fresco blues bands and BBQs in summer. ⏱ 1 hr. 632 Baltimore Pike (Rte. 1), Chadds Ford. ☎ 610/388-6221. www.chaddsford. com. Tues–Sat 10am–6pm (tastings from noon on), Sun noon–6pm.

❿ ★★ Terrain. This parklike, Urban Outfitters–owned garden center sells everything from tiny succulents to major trees, with plenty of organic lotions and shelter finds in between, plus organic meals in the Garden Café. ⏱ 1 hr. 914 Baltimore Pike, Glen Mills. ☎ 610/459-2400. www.shopterrain.com. Mon–Sat 9am–6pm (8pm in summer), Sun 9am–5pm (7pm in summer).

The Best of Lancaster County

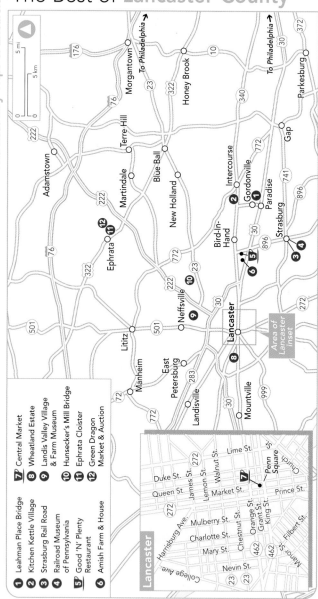

Lancaster

1 Leahman Place Bridge
2 Kitchen Kettle Village
3 Strasburg Rail Road
4 Railroad Museum of Pennsylvania
5 Good 'N' Plenty Restaurant
6 Amish Farm & House
7 Central Market
8 Wheatland Estate
9 Landis Valley Village & Farm Museum
10 Hunsecker's Mill Bridge
11 Ephrata Cloister
12 Green Dragon Market & Auction

Though less than 60 miles from Philadelphia, farm-rich Lancaster County feels worlds away. This is mostly because of the thousands of Old Order Amish and Mennonite residents who live off the land in a devout fashion that shuns modern ways, choosing horse-and-buggies over cars, nature over technology, plain over fancy. *Tip:* Rte. 340 is more scenic than busy Rte. 30. START: **PA Turnpike (76-W) to Rte. 30; the drive should take approx. 1 hr. during non-rush-hour times.**

1 ★ Leahman Place Bridge. Also known as Eshleman's Mill or Paradise Bridge, this painted-red covered wooden bridge stands amid cornfields and farms, a pastoral introduction to a pastoral region. Drive slowly: There's only one lane, and, according to lore, a kiss along the span brings good luck. ⏱ *¼ hr. N. Belmont Rd., ½ mile north of Rte. 30 just east of Paradise.*

2 kids Kitchen Kettle Village. A first pit stop for shoppers: This friendly, countrified (and, yes, kitschy) outdoor mall has a few dozen vendors of quilts, crafts, homemade jams, relishes, and ice creams. ⏱ *1/2 hr. 3529 Old Philadelphia Pike (Rte. 340), Intercourse.* ☎ *800/732-3538 or 717/768-8261. www.kitchenkettle. com. Nov–Apr Mon–Sat 9am–5pm; May–Oct Mon–Sat 9am–6pm.*

3 ★ kids Strasburg Rail Road. Book a ticket for a 45-minute ride on America's oldest short-line train

from a circa-1832 station through the countryside. Your purchase also earns you entry to train-themed amusements and attractions such as a circa-1885 switch tower, working vintage pump car, mechanical shop, and a hand-propelled 1930s "cranky car." On occasion, a full-size Thomas-brand tank engine shows up to offer rides to young fans. On other occasions, the trains offer wine and cheese rides for more mature riders. ⏱ *1½ hr. Rte. 741-East, Strasburg.* ☎ *717/687-7522. www.strasburgrailroad.com. $14–$25 adults, $8–$25 children 3–11. Hours vary wildly, but roughly: May–Aug daily 11am–6 or 7pm; Apr and Sept-Oct Mon–Fri noon–4pm, Sat–Sun 11am–7pm; Nov–Dec and Feb–Mar most Sat–Sun (and some Mon) noon–2 or 3pm.*

4 kids Railroad Museum of Pennsylvania. Want more trains? Cross the street to this history-rich

The 45-minute ride on the Strasburg Rail Road departs from a circa-1832 station.

display, where dozens of stationary engines tell the tale of America's preferred transit of yore. ① ½ hr. *Rtes. 896 & 741-East, Strasburg.* ☎ *717/687-8628. www.rrmuseumpa. org. Admission $10 adults, $9 seniors, $8 children 3–11. Daily 9am–5pm, Sun noon–5pm (Nov–Mar closed Mon).*

5 Stick-to-yer-ribs country fare is the name of the game in these parts. Diners sit at tables for 10 or 12 to dig into family-style fried chicken, chow chow, and shoofly pie at ★ **Good 'N' Plenty Restaurant.** *Rte. 896 (btw. Rtes. 340 and 30), Smoketown.* ☎ *717/394-7111. www.goodnplenty.com. $$.*

6 ★ **kids** **Amish Farm & House.** Outsiders (or "English") are, respectfully, unwelcome trespassers upon Amish farms, and inside Amish homes or schoolhouses. The next best thing is to visit this facsimile thereof. This attraction's location—sandwiched between a Target and a strip mall—may seem odd, but tune out the suburban surroundings, and the experience feels sublimely

The replica Amish Farm & House feels sublimely authentic.

authentic. Basic admission includes access to a 204-year-old, 10-room formerly Amish-owned house, a newer one-room schoolhouse, old covered bridge, and 15-acre farm with live animals. ① 1½ hr. *2395 Lincoln Hwy. at Witmer Rd., east of Lancaster.* ☎ *717/394-6185. www. amishfarmandhouse.com. Admission $9 adults, $8 seniors, $6 children 5–11. Apr–May & Sept–Oct daily 9am–5pm; June–Aug daily 9am–6pm; Nov–Mar daily 10am–4pm.*

7 ★★ **Central Market.** In the heart of Lancaster, the nation's oldest farmer's market—housed in a stunning Romanesque Revival building—offers 80 stalls of local delicacies, from sweet bologna and shoofly pie to scrapple, schnitzel and whoopie pies. *23 N. Market St., Lancaster.* ☎ *717/735-6890. www. centralmarketlancaster.com. $–$$. Open Tues & Fri 6am–4pm, Sat 6am–2pm.*

8 ★ **Wheatland Estate.** Two miles west of Lancaster is the gracious Federal mansion and arboretum of James Buchanan, the 15th U.S. president. Costumed guides offer hour-long tours. ① 1 hr. *230 North President Ave (at Marietta Ave./Rte. 23) Lancaster.* ☎ *717/392-4633. www.lancasterhistory.org. Admission $10 adults, $8 seniors & students, free 10 and under. Apr–Oct Mon–Sat 10am–4pm; Feb–Mar Fri–Sat 10am–4pm; Nov–Dec by appt.*

9 ★★ **Landis Valley Village & Farm Museum.** Costumed re-enactors scattered amid 40 historic structures bring traditional, old-time Dutch country living to life in this complex just 2½ miles northeast of Lancaster. Displays and demonstrations highlight what everyday life was like for PA's rural German communities from 1740 to

1940. It's far less cheesy and more informative than similar, historically costumed theme parks masquerading as Colonial-era infotainment. The heirloom seed project is downright academic (and makes for great gifts for gardeners). Once or twice a month, Hands-on History Days let the family try their hands at ye olde chores, from churning butter to punching tin to cooking on an open hearth. ⏱ *1½ hr. 2451 Kissel Hill Road, Lancaster.* ☎ *717/569-0401. www.landisvalleymuseum.org. Admission $12 adults, $10 seniors, $8 ages 2–11. Mon–Sat 9am–5pm, Sun noon–5pm.*

🔟 Hunsecker's Mill Bridge. Photo op! The country's longest single-span covered bridge (180 ft) divides two townships and turns Hunsecker Road into Hunsicker Road. Think of it as Lancaster's

Landis Valley Village & Farm offers a glimpse of rural life from 1740 to 1940.

version of the equator. ⏱ *¼ hr. Hunsicker Rd. just west of Mondale Rd and Snake Hill Rd. (1 mile southeast of Rte. 272; 1/2 mile north of Rte. 23), Upper Leacock & Manheim townships.*

⓫ ★ Ephrata Cloister. Like the Pyramids, the austere structures of this 18th-century society were built with nary a nail. In the 1720s, Conrad Beissel moved from Germany to Pennsylvania to establish a monastic version of Christianity. Unfortunately, Beissel's rules about celibacy weren't a strong selling feature. He died in 1768, and the cloister's members soon became German Seventh Day Adventists. See how these folks lived, alone and apart. Pay special detail to their beautiful *frakturschriften* (calligraphy used in printmaking), pottery, and book binding. ⏱ *1½ hr. 633 W. Main St., Ephrata (near junction of rtes. 272 & 322).* ☎ *717/733-6600. www.ephratacloister.org. Admission $10 adults, $9 seniors, $6 ages 3–11. Apr–Oct Mon–Sat 9am–5pm, Sun noon–5pm; Mar & Nov–Dec Tues–Sat 9am–5pm, Sun noon–5pm; Jan–Feb Wed–Sat 9am–5pm, Sun noon–5pm.*

⓬ Market & Auction. If it's Friday, make sure you stop at this super giant, super authentic spread of 400 stalls manned by growers, merchants, and artisans; an auction house for hay and small animals, and (weather permitting) an outdoor flea market and arcade. It's a true taste of rural America, Pennsylvania Dutch–style. (And you just might find yourself driving home with a gal named "Bessy" in tow.) ⏱ *1 hr. 955 N. State St. (at Garden Spot Rd.).* ☎ *717/738-1117. www. greendragonmarket.com. Fri 9am–9pm.*

The Best of Bucks & Montgomery Counties

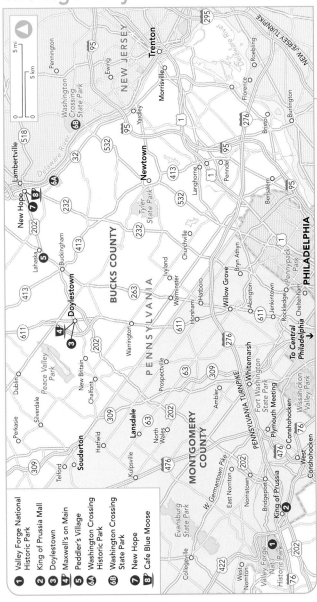

1 Valley Forge National Historic Park
2 King of Prussia Mall
3 Doylestown
4 Maxwell's on Main
5 Peddler's Village
6A Washington Crossing Historic Park
6B Washington Crossing State Park
7 New Hope
8 Cafe Blue Moose

wo iconic moments of the American Revolution occurred in these neighboring counties at the city's northern doorstep: The brutal winter camp at Valley Forge, and Washington's crossing of the Delaware. The region is home to the quaint shops of Peddler's Village and the largest mall in America. Doylestown has bustling streets lined with cafes, Victorian houses, quirky museums, and a home-grown castle. Star-studded plays often test their chops in hip, riverside New Hope before moving to Broadway. START: **Take I-76 21 miles north to Valley Forge (or city buses 125 & 139; there's also a SEPTA train to Doylestown).**

Valley Forge National Historic Park was built around Washington's stone house.

1 ★★ Valley Forge National Historic Park. In 1893, PA created its first state park around the trim stone house where Washington rode out the bitter winter of 1777–78, mulling over recent defeats and keeping an eye on supplies lines from Reading and Lancaster—and on the British-occupied capital of Philadelphia down the road. By 1976, the National Park Service knit together 18 surrounding farms and scattered the 3,500 acres with replicas of the crude cabins that housed Washington's troops. After 6 months of unified drills in modern military techniques under veteran Prussian officer Friedrich von Steuben, this ragtag baker's dozen of former state militias—each with its own uniforms and insignia (and conflicting loyalties)—emerged as a single fighting machine: the U.S. Continental Army. ① *2 hrs. 1400 N. Outer Line Dr., King of Prussia. (where Rte. 422 crosses the PA Turnpike).* ☎ *610/783-1074. www.nps. gov/vafo. Free. Daily 7am–dark (buildings close 5pm).*

2 King of Prussia Mall. We know you didn't come to Philly to hit the mall, but if you're feeling peckish and forgot to pack a picnic, amble 3 miles southeast to the 40 restaurants (and 400 stores) of this mega-mall. Due respect to Minnesota's vaunted Mall of America, this actually *is* the country's largest shopping complex as measured by actual retail space (3 million sq ft). ① *½ hr. 160 N. Guelph Rd. (where I-76, PA 202, and the PA Turnpike cross).* ☎ *610/265-5727. www. kingofprussiamall.com. Mon–Sat 10am–9pm, Sun 11am–6pm.*

3 ★★★ Doylestown. Bucks' county seat—a lovely collection of Victorian homes, shops, and restaurants—has been hometown to notables from Margaret Mead and Oscar Hammerstein to Pearl S.

Buck and P!nk. Two in particular left their mark. Colorful examples from Henry Mercer's (1856–1930) Moravian Tile Works decorate his wacky poured-cement Fonthill Castle on the edge of town (book ahead for the required tour). Downtown, he poured the Mercer Museum, a treasure trove of everyday Americana—think: Grandma's attic re-imagined by M.C. Escher, six stories of hidden rooms, meandering halls, and secret staircases zigzagging crazily around an impressive open atrium, all packed with 40,000 pre-industrial objects from Franklin stoves to cider presses to Conestoga wagons. Prolific author James Michener's (1907–1997) dream of a Doylestown museum celebrating local artists became the James A. Michener Art Museum just across the street. ⏱ *3 hrs. General info: www.doylestownborough.net. Fonthill: E. Court St. & Rte. 313.* ☎ *215/ 348-9461. www.fonthillmuseum.org. $12 adults, $10 seniors, $6 ages 6–17. Tours Mon–Sat 10am–5pm, Sun noon–5pm. Mercer Museum: 84 S. Pine St.* ☎ *215/345-0210. www.mercermuseum.org. $12 adults, $10 seniors, $6 ages 6–17. Mon–Sat 10am–5pm, Sun noon–5pm. Michener: 138 S. Pine St.* ☎ *215/ 340-9800. $15 adults, $13 seniors, $11 students, $7.50 ages 6–18; Tues– Fri 10am–4:30pm, Sat 10am–5pm, Sun noon–5pm.*

The Mercer Museum is packed with 40,000 pre-industrial objects.

4 ★ **Maxwell's on Main.** This family-run restaurant in the center of town serves fabulous French toast and Eggs Bayou (Cajun-style "Benedict") at brunch; burgers, sandwiches, and inventive pizzalike flatbreads at lunch. *37 N. Main St., Doylestown.* ☎ *215/340-1880. www.momsmaxwellsonmain.com. $–$$.*

5 **Peddler's Village.** Ye olde strip mall, a conglomeration of 70 shops—heavy on the gifts and crafts—and a half-dozen restaurants in a brick-paved country-town setting. ⏱ *1 hr. At Rtes. 202 and 263, Lahaska.* ☎ *215/794-4051. www. peddlersvillage.com. Mon–Thurs 10m–6pm, Fri–Sat 10am–9pm, Sun 11am–6pm.*

6 ★ **Washington's Crossing.** Following a string of defeats, the Patriot cause was at its lowest ebb in December 1776. Most army contracts were up, the weary troops ready to go home—until George Washington entreated them to stick it out for one last campaign. On a frigid Christmas Eve, under cover of darkness as a driving rain turned to sleet and snow, Washington and 2,400 troops silently crossed the ice-chocked Delaware River in Durham Boats (normally used to transport pig iron) from Pennsylvania to Johnson's Ferry, NJ. They marched to Trenton, surprising the Hessian troops stationed there. After a brief battle—in which the Americans lost

Country Sleepovers

With towns named Paradise and Lititz, who wouldn't want to spend the night? For a romantic B&B in the heart of Lititz's historic district, book the modernized 1850 Federal-style manse of the ★★ **Alden House** (62 E. Main St.; ☎ 800/584-0753 or 717/627-3363; www.aldenhouse.com; 7 units; doubles $109–$159; AE, DISC, MC, V). Guests choose from modern or traditional suites—from Jacuzzis to stained-glass windows—in the two vintage homes that comprise ★★ **The Inns at Doneckers** (318–324 N. State St., near rtes. 322 and 222, Ephrata; ☎ 800/377-2206 or 717/738-9502; 31 units; doubles $75–$250; AE, DC, DISC, MC, V). Favorite rooms at the ★ **Best Western Revere Inn** include the modern suites in the 1790 farmhouse (3063 Lincoln Hwy./Rte. 30, Paradise; ☎ 800/429-7383 or 717/687-8601; www.revereinn.com; 94 units; doubles $80–$130 w/breakfast; AE, DC, DISC, MC, V). A great outdoor pool, playground, and pet-friendly policies make the ★ **Historic Strasburg Inn** (1400 Historic Dr., Strasburg; ☎ 717/687-7691; www.historicinnofstrasburg.com; 102 units; doubles $100–$120; AE, DC, DISC, MC, V) a great hotel for the whole family.

just two men (among the 5 wounded: future president James Monroe)—the Hessians surrendered. Though small, this victory boosted military morale and public sentiment, and led to a string of Patriot victories at the Second Battle of Trenton (Jan 2), then Princeton (Jan 3), and Cowpens (Jan 17). The tide of the war began to turn.

There are interpretive parks on both sides of the river. On the PA side are the 500 acres and 13 historic buildings of **6A Washington Crossing Historic Park,** including McConkey's Ferry Inn, where Washington dined and made the final plans for the daring crossing. On the NJ side is the 3,575-acre **6B Washington Crossing State Park,** laced with 15 miles of hiking trails, a museum and visitor center, the historic Johnson Ferry House likely used by Washington, and an open-air theater for summer plays and Monday-night movies

(www.dpacatoat.com). ⏱ *1 hr. Washington Crossing Historic Park, PA: 1112 River Rd., Washington Crossing, PA.* ☎ *215/493-4076. www.ushistory.org/washington crossing. Historic buildings $6; outdoor park free. Mar 10–Dec Tues– Sun 10am–4pm (outdoor park open year-round daily 8am–dusk). Washington Crossing State Park, NJ: 355 Washington Crossing-Pennington Road, Titusville, NJ.* ☎ *609/737-0623. www.state.nj.us/dep/parksand forests. Free except $7 ($5 NJ residents) vehicle charge Memorial Day– Labor Day. Daily 8am–4:30pm (Visitors Center Museum: 9am–4pm).*

7 ★★ New Hope. This pre-Revolutionary ferry depot on the Delaware River (once home to Colonial hothead Aaron Burr) grew into an art colony in the early 1900s, a gay Mecca in the 1950s, and remains a thriving summer-home spot and tourist destination. Its renowned

Bucks County Playhouse (www.bcptheater.org)—recently reborn from bankruptcy—boasts a surprising pedigree of A-listers (Sigourney Weaver and David Hyde Pierce recently tread the boards) and premieres from the likes of Neil Simon and Terrence McNally fine-tuning Broadway-bound productions. The town also anchors one end of the Ivyland Railroad, a 45-minute round-trip steam train loop to Lahaska (see bullet ❺) made famous in the 1914 *Perils of Pauline* cliffhanger serials (picture: a villain twirling his mustache; a damsel tied to the tracks; will our hero save her in time?). ⏲ *2 hrs. General info: www.newhopevisitorscenter.org and www.visitnewhope.com. Ivyland R&R: 32 W. Bridge St.* ☎ *215/862-2332. www.newhoperailroad.com. From $19 adults, $17 ages 2–11, $4 1 and under. Hourly runs daily late May–Oct, weekends in winter.*

8 ★ **Cafe Blue Moose.** Innovative BYOB run by local teens—though the chef-owner is now a seasoned 21-year-old—with French-inflected European prix-fixe menus ($22 for 2 courses, $27 for 3). *9 W. Mechanic St., New Hope.* ☎ *215/862-6800. www.cafebluemoose.com. Wed–Sun dinner; Sun brunch. No credit cards. $–$$.* ●

Before You Go

Official Tourist Information

Independence Visitor Center (1 Independence Mall West, at 6th & Market sts.; ☎ 800/537-7676; www. phlvisitorcenter.com and www. uwushunu.com). Other tourist office locations: in **Sister Cities Park Café,** 200 N. 18th St. at the Benjamin Franklin Parkway; in **City Hall,** Broad & Market sts. (☎ 215/686-2840); in the **Convention Center,** 1101 Arch St.; and in **Love Park,** 1599 JFK Blvd. at 16th St. (☎ 215/683-0246). Also handy: **Greater Philadelphia Tourism Marketing** (www.visitphilly.com); **Philadelphia Convention and Visitors Bureau** (1700 Market St., Ste. 3000; ☎ 800/225-5745 or 215/636-3300; www.discoverphl.com); **Visit Pennsylvania** (☎ 800/847-4872; www.visitpa.com); official events guides/blogs www.phillyfunguide.com and www.uwushunu.com.

The Best Time to Go

Summer is the height of tourism season, especially around historic attractions. Late July through August, be prepared to swelter in line for Independence Hall. (On the other hand, summer is the best time to score a table at a trendy restaurant.) Fall and winter offer the lowest prices on hotel rooms. Spring weather is often peculiar—hot one day, chilly the next—but late May and early June are usually best for garden buffs. Times to avoid: During the University of Pennsylvania's graduation in mid-May.

Festivals and Special Events

JAN. New Year's Day means the odd, debauched, daylong **Mummer's Parade** (☎ 215/336-3050; www.mummers.com) along Broad Street.

FEB. Mid-to-late month, Chinatown pops and sparkles with a **Chinese New Year celebration** (☎ 215/922-2156; chinatown-pcdc.org) on its streets and in its restaurants.

MAR. The **Philadelphia Flower Show** (☎ 215/988-8800; www.theflowershow.com) is the largest indoor exhibit of its kind. Go early for the freshest displays. Expect crowds.

APR. For 3 days, 22,000 of the best college, high school, and track club runners from 60 countries (and 100,000 spectators) descend upon Franklin Field for the exuberant Penn Relays (☎ 215/898-6151; www.thepennrelays.com), the country's largest and oldest track-and-field meet with some 425 races over 35 hours.

MAY On a (hopefully) sunny Saturday, some 50,000 celebrants turn out for the **Rittenhouse Row Spring Festival** (www.rittenhouserow.org), a block party gone chic, thanks to dozens of outdoor kiosks offering haute cuisine and sublime shopping.

JUNE Early in the month, bars and breweries host beer-centric events for the **Philly Beer Week** (www.phillybeerweek.org) showcasing suds both local and exotic. There's no better place to celebrate **Flag Day** (June 14) than Old City's Betsy Ross House (☎ 215/629-4026; www.betsyrosshouse.org).

JULY The city where the Declaration of Independence was written celebrates **Independence Week**

Previous page: Tourists ride Segway i2 Gliders near the Philadelphia Museum of Art.

(the week of July 4) at just about every venue—notably, of course, at the historic sights around Independence Mall—with historical re-enactments, outdoor movies, ice cream socials, and concerts and performances galore, culminating in fireworks over Penn's Landing and the Philadelphia Museum of Art.

AUG. The Reading Terminal Market's weeklong **Pennsylvania Dutch Festival** (☎ 215/922-2317; www. readingterminalmarket.org) features quilts, music, crafts, and shoofly pie.

SEPT. Inspired by the cutting-edge Scottish arts extravaganza of the same name, the **Philadelphia Live Arts Festival and Philly Fringe Festival** (☎ 215/413-9006; www.livearts-fringe.org) offers 2 weeks in early September of experimental theater and more in and beyond Old City.

OCT. All manner of fine artists let the public into their workspaces during the two-weekends-long **Philadelphia Open Studio Tours** (☎ 215/546-7775; www.philaopen studios.org).

NOV. **Philadelphia Museum of Art Craft Show** (☎ 215/684-7930; pmacraftshow.org) shows off the work of local and international artisans in the Convention Center.

DEC. The biggest, most historic of military sporting events, the **Army-Navy game** (☎ 877/TIX-ARMY or 800/US-4-NAVY; armynavygame. com) is a grand tradition come early December. So is the **holiday light and music show**—a rite of passage among local kids—at Macy's in the old John Wanamaker Building (☎ 215/241-9000; www.

macys.com)—as well as its postmodern cousin, the **Comcast Centers Holiday Spectacular audio-visual extravaganza** at 1701 JFK Blvd.

The Weather
Philadelphia's mid-Atlantic climate produces cold and often gray winters, cool and sometimes rainy springs, hot and typically humid summers, and mild and crisp falls. Just like the seasons in kids' books.

Restaurant and Theater Reservations
Though a few notable BYOB restaurants are first-come, first-served, most larger restaurants accept reservations by phone or via the Internet at **Open Table** (www. opentable.com). For performances by the Philadelphia Orchestra, the Pennsylvania Ballet, Philadelphia Chamber Music Society, and at the Kimmel Center for the Performing Arts, Academy of Music, Mann, Merriam, and others, the telephone box office is **Ticket Philadelphia** (☎ 215/893-1999; www.ticket philadelphia.org). The city's non-profit box office **Upstages** (☎ 215/569-9700) represents a handful of smaller companies and theaters.

Car Rentals
Most major renters maintain offices at Philadelphia International Airport, and there are a small number of cars available from 30th Street Station and at Center City kiosks. Check out www.rentalcars.com—or any number of travel websites—for car-rental discounts. (See p 172 for contact information.)

Getting **There**

By Plane
Philadelphia International Airport (PHL; ☎ 800/745-4283 or

215/937-6937; www.phl.org) is the city's major airport, about 10 miles southwest of Center City. A **SEPTA** train (☎ 215/580-7800; www.septa.com) runs every 30 minutes to town ($7 adults one-way). A taxi costs about $30, including tip.

By Car
I-95 runs north and south along the city's eastern edge. The Pennsylvania Turnpike (I-276) cuts east-west through the city's northern suburbs. I-76 (aka the Schuylkill Expwy.) runs southeast to northwest, connecting to Center City via the Vine Street Expressway (I-676). I-476 (aka the Blue Rte.) connects all of the above via western suburbs, about 15 miles west of town, linking I-276 and I-76 at the north, and I-95 to the south.

By Train
Amtrak (☎ 800/872-7245; www.amtrak.com) runs to 30th Street Station (at Market St., in West Philly just over the Schuylkill River from Center City), where you can pick up

a cab to your hotel, or connect to subways or regional rail (SEPTA) lines.

By Bus
Greyhound/Peter Pan buses arrive at the **Greyhound Bus Terminal** (10th and Filbert sts.; ☎ 800/231-2222 or 215-931-4075; www.greyhound.com).

BoltBus (www.boltbus.com), travels to and from NYC and Boston; its stop in Philly is on JFK Blvd. 100 yards west of 30th St. (near 30th St. train station).

Megabus (www.megabus.com) goes to and from a dozen destinations—including NYC, Boston, Washington, Baltimore, Pittsburgh, and Toronto—from a stop on JFK Blvd. 200 yards west of 30th Street Station (with a second stop, for NYC service only, on Independence Mall).

Getting **Around**

On Foot
Center City measures 25 blocks (2 miles) from east to west and 12 blocks (1mile) north to south. A pedestrian should be able to cross town in about an hour and cross Old City in 15 minutes.

By Car
Two-thirds of all visitors to Philadelphia arrive by car. Traffic into town can be congested, especially during rush hours. The majority of Center City's streets are one-way, and some open up to three lanes during rush hour, so pay close attention to street signs. For info on garages, lots, and parking meters, check out the official www.philapark.org.

By Taxi
Base fare for cabs is $2.70 and 23¢ for each additional 1/10 mile. A cross-town trip should cost about $11. Two good operators are **Olde City Taxi** (☎ 215/338-0838) and **Quaker City** (☎ 215/728-8000), although hailing from a street corner is usually fastest.

By Public Transportation
SEPTA (☎ 215/580-7800; www.septa.com) operates all public transit, including buses that run along most major streets; trolleys; and subways that run beneath Market and Broad streets (use the Broad Street Line if you're headed to a sporting event or concert at a stadium in South Philadelphia; it's much faster and cheaper than driving).

Note that between 2013 and 2015, SEPTA will be (slowly) rolling out its new ticketless NPT system, which will use pre-paid tap-and-go cards and cellphones to pay fares. Until then, all fares are $2 cash (exact change required)—or $1.55 if you purchase tokens from a sidewalk kiosk or train station (in packs of 2, 5, or 10). An $11 1-day Independence Pass ($28 for the Family Pass for up to 5 family members, of which no more than 2 are over 18) is valid for unlimited rides on any SEPTA bus, subway, trolley, Phlash bus, the Airport line, and regional rail arriving in Center City after 9:30am. A $7 One Day Convenience Pass is valid for eight trips on buses, subways, and trolleys on 1 day (not valid for regional rail).

By Tourist Bus

The purple, daytime-only **Phlash buses** (☎ 215/389-8687; www.phillyphlash.com) loop around 19 attractions every 15 minutes—but only Memorial Day through Labor Day (plus Fri–Sun in May, Sept, and Oct). Fare is $2 per ride.

Philadelphia Trolley Works (☎ 215/389-8687; www.phillytour.com) operates double-decker bus and Victorian-style trolley tours with 21 stops; an all-day pass is $27 adults, $10 children.

Fast **Facts**

APARTMENT RENTALS Short-term: Try www.airbnb.com, www.vrbo.com, or www.rentalo.com. **Long-term:** Try www.craigslist.org or the alt weekly newspapers, *Philadelphia Weekly* (www.philadelphiaweekly.com) and *City Paper* (www.citypaper.net).

AREA CODES In **Philadelphia:** 215 and 267. In the **Pennsylvania suburbs:** 610 and 484. In **southern New Jersey:** 856 and 609.

ATMS Throughout the city, most banks and convenience stores offer 24-hour ATMs, most charging a $2 to $4 fee per usage if the machine does not belong to your own bank. *Tip:* Call it a "Mac machine" and they'll think you're a local.

BABYSITTING Hotel concierges are your best source.

BANKING HOURS Most banks are open weekdays 6am to 5pm; TD Bank (formerly Commerce; www.tdbank.com) is open weekdays 7:30am to 8pm, Saturday 7:30am to 6pm, and Sunday 11am to 4pm.

B&BS Try **Bed & Breakfast Connections of Philadelphia** (☎ 800/448-3619; www.bnbphiladelphia.com), or visit www.bedandbreakfast.com or www.airbnb.com.

BIKE RENTALS Breakaway Bikes, 1923 Chestnut St. (☎ 215/568-6002; www.breakawaybikes.com) rents hybrids ($10/hour, $50 /day) from its shop Monday to Saturday 10am to 7pm, Sunday noon to 5pm. **Wheel Fun Rentals** (www.wheelfunrentals.com) rents bikes ($12/hour or $38/day) and surreys at several locations whenever it's sunny and over 55°F: by the Independence Hall Visitors Center at 1 North Independence Mall West (☎ 215/523-5827; daily 8:30am–6pm); 1 Boathouse Row behind the Art Museum (☎ 215/232-7778; 9am–Sunset Apr–May weekends and summer daily; 10am–Sunset Sept–Oct daily, Apr–May weekdays, and Nov–Mar weekends); Capriccio at Cafe Cret at 110 N. 16th Street (☎ 215/735-9797; Mon–Fri

6:30am–7pm, Sat–Sun 8am–8pm); and at the Trolley Car Cafe at 3269 S. Ferry Road in East Fairmount Park (☎ 215/385-6703; Apr–Oct 7am–8pm).

BUSINESS HOURS Most shops and restaurants are open Monday to Saturday 10am to 6 or 7pm, Sunday noon to 6pm. Offices are usually open weekdays 9am to 5pm.

CLIMATE See Weather.

CONCERTS See Theater Tickets.

CONSULATES AND EMBASSIES Chile, the Czech Republic, the Dominican Republic, Germany, Israel, and Italy all have consulates in Philadelphia. The closest locations for most other foreign consulates are Washington, D.C. or New York City. Find yours: www.embassyworld.com.

DENTISTS See Emergencies.

DOCTORS See Emergencies.

EMBASSIES See Consulates and Embassies.

EMERGENCIES For fire, police, and medical emergencies, dial ☎ 911. The nonemergency number for the police is ☎ 311. For poison control, dial ☎ 800/222-1222 or 215/386-2100. For dental emergencies ☎ 866/685-2008 or 215/545-2600 (www.emergencydentist247.com).

EVENT LISTINGS Check out the daily newspapers the *Philadelphia Inquirer* and the *Philadelphia Daily News,* and their joint Web site (www.philly.com). The *Philadelphia Weekly* is available free from corner boxes and publishes on Wednesday (www.philadelphiaweekly.com). The *City Paper* is available free from corner boxes and publishes Thursday (www.citypaper.net). Monthly *Philadelphia Magazine* and its website (www.phillymag.com) are also a great source of info. *Greater Philadelphia Cultural Alliance*'s website, www.phillyfunguide. com, is also a good resource.

FAMILY TRAVEL For family travel info, visit the **Greater Philadelphia Tourism Marketing Corporation** (www.visitphilly.com); don't miss The Philadelphia Pass for family discounts on admission (www.philadelphiapass.com).

GAY & LESBIAN TRAVELERS Center City is welcoming to GLBT residents and visitors. The neighborhoods of Midtown and Washington West, a.k.a. the "gayborhood" (especially between Broad and 12th sts., Walnut and Spruce sts.) have a concentration of gay-owned, -operated, and -friendly businesses. The *Philadelphia Gay News* (www.epgn. com) is available from sidewalk boxes. Also handy: www.facebook. com/VisitGayPhilly. For support groups and events, contact the William Way Community Center, 1315 Spruce St. (☎ 215/732-2220, www. waygay.org).

HEALTH CLUBS **Sweat Gym** (www. sweatfitness.com) offers day passes for $15 at nine locations, including 1425 Arch St. (☎ 215/546-0303); 200 S. 24th St. (☎ 215/351-0100); 45 N. 3rd St. (☎ 215/923-8763); and 700 Passyunk Ave. (☎ 215/627-5600). **Philadelphia Sports Clubs** (www.mysportsclubs.com) offers day passes for $25 at 250 S. 5th St. (☎ 215/592-8900); 1735 Market St. (☎ 215/564-5353); and 2000 Hamilton St. (☎ 215/568-9555).

HOLIDAYS Public and observed: January 1 (New Year's Day), third Monday in January (Martin Luther King, Jr. Day), third Monday in February (Washington's Birthday), last Monday in May (Memorial Day), July 4 (Independence Day), first Monday in September (Labor Day), November 11 (Veteran's Day), fourth Thursday in November (Thanksgiving), December 25 (Christmas).

HOSPITALS **Philadelphia Children's Hospital,** 34th Street and

Useful Websites

www.phlvisitorcenter.com The city's official portal for visitors, also the place to reserve tickets to Independence Hall and for the basics for a short visit.

www.visitphilly.com A more comprehensive guide to Philadelphia and the surrounding Pennsylvania counties, created by the region's premier promoters—also great for hotel discounts. Also check out their www.uwishunu.com insider's blog.

www.discoverphl.com The site for the Philadelphia Conventions & Visitors Bureau, packed with useful info.

www.phila.gov Straight from local government, this less-frequently updated website has useful info nonetheless.

www.philly.com The *Philadelphia Inquirer* and the *Philadelphia Daily News,* the city's two major newspapers, are the best and fastest sources for local news and events.

www.phillyfunguide.com An arts and events site maintained by the Greater Philadelphia Cultural Alliance.

www.phillymag.com The site for the monthly *Philadelphia* magazine offers local insider stories and great editorials on shopping, dining, and events.

www.visitpa.com The official Pennsylvania state tourism site.

Civic Center Boulevard (☎ 215/590-1000; www.chop.edu); **University of Pennsylvania Hospital,** 3400 Spruce St. (☎ 800/789-7366; www.pennhealth.com); **Pennsylvania Hospital,** 8th and Spruce streets (☎ 215/829-3000; www.pennhealth.com/pahosp); **Thomas Jefferson University Hospital,** 11th and Walnut streets (☎ 215/955-6000; www.jeffersonhospital.org).

INSURANCE Check your existing policies (and credit cards) before purchasing insurance to cover trip cancellation, lost luggage, medical expenses, medical evacuation, or car rental. There are more than two-dozen travel insurance specialists, so the best way to comparison shop policies is to use an aggregator that specializes in comparing all available policies at the same time: www.insuremytrip.com or www.squaremouth.com.

INTERNET Most coffee shops offer free wireless Internet access. The **Connect Philly initiative** (ph.ly/connect) helps you find local free Wi-Fi hotspots (and libraries with terminals) via text message by texting any Philadelphia address or intersection to 215/240-7296; you will receive a list of nearby locations. For computer kiosks, try branches of the **Free Library of Philadelphia** (☎ 215/686-5322; www.freelibrary.org) or the **Capital One 360 Café** at 17th and Walnut streets (☎ 215/731-1410; cafes.capitalone360.com).

LAUNDROMATS **U-Do-It Laundry & Dry Cleaning** is at 1513 Spruce St. (☎ 215/735-1255; www.udoitlaundry.com; open daily 7am–9pm). **Quick & Clean Coin Laundry** is at 320 S. 10th St., between Spruce and Pine streets (no phone; open daily 8am–8pm).

What Things Cost in Philadelphia

A cup of coffee from La Colombe	$1.75
Subway, bus, or trolley fare	$2
A pint of Yards ale at Standard Tap	$4–$5
Cheesesteak at Pat's King of Steaks	$7.50
Adult admission to the Philadelphia Museum of Art	$20
A standing-room-only Phillies ticket	$14–$20
Taxi ride from airport to Center City, with tip	$30
Train ride from airport to Center City	$7
Dinner for two at Ralph's Italian Restaurant	$65
Average double hotel room, one night (before tax)	$149

LIMOS **Dave's Best Limousine** (☎ 215/288-1000; www.davesbest limoservice.com); **Executive Town-car** (☎ 215/485-7265; www.philly-sedan.com); **Victory Limo** (☎ 610/365-4100; www.victorylimo.net).

LOST PROPERTY, CREDIT CARDS For **American Express,** call ☎ 800/528-4800. For **MasterCard,** call ☎ 800/627-8372 or 636/722-7111. For **Visa,** call ☎ 800/847-2911 or 410/581-9994. For other credit cards, call this directory: ☎ 800/555-1212.

LOST PROPERTY At the airport: Check with the Communications Center at the Philadelphia International Airport, Departures Roadway, between Terminals C and D (☎ 610/521-7206; www.phl.org). On public transit: If you've lost an item on a SEPTA bus, subway, or trolley, call ☎ 215/580-7800; on SEPTA Regional Rail, call ☎ 215/580-5740.

MAIL & POSTAGE At press time, domestic postage rates are 33¢ for a postcard, 46¢ for a letter. Find post offices and international rates at www.usps.gov.

PARKING On-street parking is notoriously complicated, with zoned neighborhood permits, regulations that change according to the day and hour, and a diminishing number of coin-operated parking meters—the city is slowly moving toward a block-by-block payment via automated ticket kiosks. Parking garages abound, but are not cheap: Expect to pay around $24 to $30 per day. More info: www.philapark.org.

PASSES **Philadelphia Citypass** (www.citypass.com) offers admission to five attractions (2 of which involve a choice): the Franklin Institute, Adventure Aquarium, Philadelphia Trolley Works tour, and either the National Constitution Center or the Zoo, and the Eastern State Penitentiary or the Please Touch Museum. It costs $59 adults, $39 children 2 to 12. Its tickets are valid 9 days from first usage. The **Philadelphia Pass** (www.philadelphia pass.com) gets you free entry to more than 40 attractions and tours—from the Art Museum to the Duck Boats—and a few other discounts (on sights, shopping, and dining) for a set period of time. It costs $49 ($39 for kids aged 2–12) for 1 day; $80 ($65 kids) for 2 days; $100 ($80 kids) for 3 days; or $115 ($95 kids) for 5 days.

PASSPORTS Virtually every traveler entering the U.S. must show a passport. U.S. and Canadian citizens by land or sea from within the Western Hemisphere may present government-issued proof of citizenship, although a passport is recommended.

PHARMACIES For 24-hour service, go to **CVS,** 1826 Chestnut St., at 19th Street (☎ 215/972-0909; www. cvs.com); or **Rite Aid** at 2301 Walnut St. at 23rd St. (☎ 215/636-9634; www.riteaid.com), or 1638 Chestnut St. at 16th St. (☎ 215/972-0234; www.riteaid.com).

SAFETY Although Center City is generally quite safe, it is not without its muggings and purse-snatchings. The northerly neighborhoods of Northern Liberties, Fishtown, and Fairmount are still in the artists' lofts/hipster bars phase of gentrification—which means, outside of a few busy blocks lined with bars and restaurants, many streets feel rather dicey after dark. No matter where you are: do not leave belongings unattended, especially in a cafe or restaurant, and be especially vigilant during holiday times. Use common city sense and be aware of your surroundings.

SENIOR TRAVELERS A compact downtown, vibrant cultural life, and widely available senior discounts at museums, events, and attractions make Philadelphia attractive to an increasing population of retirees and empty nesters.

SMOKING The city's smoking ban prohibits smoking on public transit and inside restaurants, cafes, hotels and hotel rooms, shops, offices, and the vast majority of bars (though a handful—generally dive bars—got exemptions). Smoking is permitted at outside tables and in most public spaces (i.e., on sidewalks, in parks). You must be 18 years old to purchase tobacco products.

SPECTATOR SPORTS All of Philadelphia's professional sports teams play at the stadiums at the south end of Broad Street (SEPTA Broad Street stop: AT&T station—though most locals, disgusted by the runaway branding, still call it the "Pattison Ave." station). Early April through early October, the Phillies play baseball at Citizens Bank Park (philadelphia.phillies.mlb.com). Mid-September through early January, the Eagles play football at Lincoln Financial Field (www. philadelphiaeagles.com). October through April, the Flyers play ice hockey at the Wells Fargo Center (flyers.nhl.com). Late October through mid-April, the 76ers play basketball at the Wells Fargo Center (www.nba.com/sixers).

STUDENT TRAVEL There are more colleges and universities in and around Philadelphia than in any other city in the country (depending on how you define "area," there are between 50 and 80—easily double that of Boston), so students will find a warm reception from area vendors and sights. A valid student ID will get you reduced rates on cultural sites, accommodations, car rentals, and more. You'll also earn a deep discount at Apple Hostel (formerly Bank Street Hostel) 32 S. Bank St. (☎ 877/275-1971), right in the center of all of Old City nightlife and, oh yes, history.

When in Philadelphia, pick up a copy of student papers such as the *Daily Pennsylvanian* (www.daily pennsylvanian.com) at the Ivy League University of Pennsylvania, 34th and Walnut streets (☎ 215/898-5000; www.upenn.edu); *The Temple News* (www.temple-news. com) at Temple University, North Broad Street (☎ 215/204-7000; www.temple.edu); or *The Triangle* (www.thetriangle.org) at Drexel

Philadelphia Neighborhoods

CENTER CITY In other cities, this busy central business neighborhood would be called "downtown." From east to west, the Schuylkill and Delaware rivers bind this easy-to-navigate main city section. South Street and Vine Street bind it to the south and north. Neighborhoods within this area include Old City, Society Hill, Rittenhouse Square, and Washington Square West. It is also used to refer to just the grid of streets right around City Hall.

FAIRMOUNT Also known as the Art Museum area, this neighborhood stretches north from the Benjamin Franklin Parkway to Girard Avenue. Although it's largely residential, Fairmount also includes the Free Library, Rodin Museum, Eastern State Penitentiary, Barnes Foundation, and the Philadelphia Art Museum itself.

OLD CITY Think New York's SoHo, but in the shadow of the Benjamin Franklin Bridge just north of Independence National Historical Park. It's an eclectic blend of 18th-century row houses, 19th-century warehouses, and 20th-century rehabs. This is now the city's hottest neighborhood with chic restaurants, bars, and boutiques set in historic buildings and storefronts.

RITTENHOUSE SQUARE This beautifully landscaped park—ringed by elegant condominiums built during the 1930s and historic mansions—illustrates the elegance, wealth, and culture of Philadelphia. Now, sleek outdoor cafes and luxury hotels line the park also.

SOCIETY HILL This heart of reclaimed 18th-century Philadelphia is loosely defined by Walnut and Lombard streets and Front and 7th streets. Today, it's a fashionable section of the old city, just south of Independence National Historical Park, where you can stroll among restored Federal, Colonial, and Georgian homes.

SOUTH PHILADELPHIA It's Rocky Balboa–meets–artist lofts and authentic *taquerías*. Three hundred years of immigration have made South Philadelphia the city's most colorful and ethnically diverse neighborhood, although the overwhelming feel is distinctly Italian (think: 1910s Calabria).

SOUTH STREET The street that is the southern border of Society Hill was the city limit in William Penn's day. Quiet by day and cruised by night, it's a colorful spot for casual dining, drinking, shopping, gallery-hopping, and getting pierced (or tattooed). The neighborhood's website is www.southstreet.com.

UNIVERSITY CITY West Philadelphia was farmland until the University of Pennsylvania moved here from 9th and Chestnut streets in the 1870s. Wander through Penn's campus for Ivy League architecture that includes an 1895 college green modeled on Oxford and Cambridge, but with Dutch gables.

University, 32nd and Chestnut streets (☎ 215/895-2000; www. drexel.edu).

TAXES At press time, Philadelphia's total retail sales tax is 8% on everything except clothing and groceries (prepared foods, such as at a restaurant, is taxed). Tax on liquor is 10%. Tax on hotel stays is 8.2%. (**Note:** Outside the city limits, the retail sales tax drops to the state level of 6%.) Most other taxes (parking, etc.) are already folded into the prices and rates quoted to the public.

TAXIS See Getting Around, By Taxi.

TELEPHONES Public telephones are few and far between these days but generally can be found at transportation hubs, such as train stations or the airport, and civic buildings. The cost for local calls varies with provider, though is usually 50¢. International calls start around $1 for 4 minutes. Some phones accept coins; others take credit cards.

TICKETS See Chapter 8, p 132.

TIPPING For servers in a restaurant and spa employees, tip 18% to 20% of the bill; taxi drivers 15% to 20% of fare; tip hotel chamber staff $2 to $3 per day; coat check $1; valet parking $1 per ride.

TOILETS Most attractions have facilities, as do restaurants and cafes. The latter often have a "customers only" usage policy, though you can often saunter into those at fast food establishments and chain cafes.

TOURIST OFFICES The main **Independence Visitor Center** is at 1 N. Independence Mall W. (6th & Market sts.), Philadelphia, PA 19106 (☎ 800/537-7676 or 215/965-7676; www.phlvisitorcenter.com). Other locations: in Sister Cities Park Café, 200 N. 18th St. at the Benjamin

Franklin Parkway; in City Hall, Broad & Market sts. (☎ 215/686-2840); in the Convention Center, 1101 Arch St.; and in Love Park, 1599 JFK Blvd. at 16th St. (☎ 215/683-0246). Also handy: www.visitphilly.com, www.discoverphl.com, www.uwushunu.com, www.phillyfunguide.com, and www.visitpa.com.

TOURS See Getting Around: By Tourist Bus (p 161) for hop-on/hop-off trolley and bus tours.

Free and Friendly Tours (☎ 877-558-9671; freeandfriendlytours.com) is exactly what it sounds like: the tours are free; you tip what you like.

Philly happens to be the hometown of the world's top scholar-led walking tour company, **Context Travel** (☎ 800/691-6036; www.contexttravel.com); its dozen or so thematic walks—from art and history to South Philly food and African American sites—are led by PhDs and other academics and come highly regarded, but they don't come cheap ($70).

You can find a variety of less-expensive city walks ($14–$65) from multiple local companies at www.viator.com.

You can support the folks at the non-profit **Historic Philadelphia,** 150 South Independence Mall West (☎ 215/629-4026; www.historicphiladelphia.org)—the ones who provide all the free costumed storytellers and re-enactors peppered around Old City—by taking one of their paid evening walks: Independence After Hours ($85, includes dinner at City Tavern and a night visit to Independence Hall) or the Tippler's Tour Colonial Pub Crawl ($40).

Horse-and-buggies gather along the south end of Independence Mall East for tours of Society Hill and Old City; prices start at $30 for 1 to 4 people; $7 per additional person (buggy seats up to 6).

How to Speak Like a Philadelphian in 10 Terms

Philly. Use only if you're a native. Otherwise, it's "Philadelphia."

Broad Street. The north-south boulevard bisecting Center City is what would be 14th Street. But never call Broad Street "14th Street." Its new tourist-friendly designation of "Avenue of the Arts" is a little suspicious, too. But "Broad" is good.

Second Street. If you're in South Philadelphia, call it "Two Street."

Front Street. Really 1st Street. Call it "Front."

Schuylkill. Pronounced "Skoo-kill," it's the river that flows by the Philadelphia Museum of Art between Martin Luther King, Jr. and Kelly drives. It's also the name for I-76, the interstate expressway running northwest-southeast along the city's western edge, then cutting east-west through South Philly.

Blue Route. I-476, which connects the suburbs and exurbs west of Philadelphia from I-95 near the airport to where the Pennsylvania Turnpike (confusingly numbered I-76 if you head west toward Pittsburgh, but I-276 headed east to New Jersey) meets the Northeast Extension (north up into the Poconos).

Passyunk Avenue. Pronounced "Pass-yunk," this one-way avenue runs diagonally south to north from Broad Street to South Street, through South Philadelphia.

Sansom Street. Pronounced "San-som," not "Samp-son." Although, if you're going to make a mistake, this is the one to make.

The Boulevard. The Roosevelt Boulevard, Route 1 North, is a high-speed thoroughfare running through Northeast Philadelphia, connecting the Schuylkill Expressway (I-76) to the Pennsylvania Turnpike, which leads to the New Jersey Turnpike.

Cheesesteak. One word. Not "cheese steak." Definitely not "Philly cheese steak."

March through November, **Ride the Ducks,** 6th and Chestnut streets (☎ 877/887-8225 or 215/227-3825; www.phillyducks.com; tickets $27 adults, $17 children 4–12) offers lighthearted, 90-minute tours of the city (and the Delaware River) in land-to-water World War II DUKW amphibious vehicles.

Philadelphia Segway Tours, in the visitors center at 1 N. Independence Mall W. (☎ 215/523-5827; philadelphia.segwaytoursbywheelfun.com) offers a 3-hour, full-city Segway tour ($80–$90) and a 1.5-hour Old City tour ($60–$70).

TRAVELERS WITH DISABILITIES Most attractions—although not all National Historic Landmarks—offer ADA-approved access to their facilities. For basic Philadelphia information, contact the **Mayor's Commission on People with Disabilities** (☎ 215/686-2798; www.phila.gov/mcpd). SEPTA buses are lift-equipped, and all major train stations have elevator access. **Art-Reach** (☎ 215/568-2115;

www.art-reach.org), a not-for-profit organization, maintains a list of more than 140 area facilities that offer access to persons with disabilities. The Philadelphia International Airport hotline for travelers with disabilities is ☎ 215/937-6700 (TDD ☎ 215/937-6755). The Independence Visitor Center publishes "Accessibilities," a brochure detailing accessible parking spots. The America the Beautiful pass (nps. gov) gives visually impaired or permanently disabled persons free lifetime entrance to federal recreation sites administered by the National Park Service.

A Brief **History**

EARLY 1600S Europeans first arrive in the Delaware Valley.

1638 Swedish settlers sail up the Delaware River on the *Key of Kalmar* and *Flying Griffin*, and take control of the land along the Schuylkill River.

1681 Charles II of England (1630–1685) signs the charter granting Quaker nobleman William Penn (1644–1718) more than 45,000 square miles of the New World, which offered religious freedom to all within.

1701 Penn issues a charter establishing Philadelphia as a city.

1731 Benjamin Franklin (1706–1790) creates America's first lending library.

1749 Benjamin Franklin creates the University of Pennsylvania.

1751 Benjamin Franklin invents the lightning rod.

1751 Benjamin Franklin and Thomas Bond (1712–1784) create the Colonies' first hospital.

1760 Benjamin Franklin invents the bifocal.

1774 The First Continental Congress petitions King George (1738–1820) for redress of colonists' grievances at Carpenters' Hall.

1775 Delegates from all 13 Colonies meet for the Second Continental Congress, after the American Revolutionary War begins.

1776 The Congress signs the United States Declaration of Independence, turning colonies into states and separating from England.

1783 The American Revolution ends.

1790 Philadelphia becomes the capital of the new United States of America.

1800 Washington, D.C., becomes the capital of the U.S.

1876 The Centennial Exposition of 1876—the first world's fair—takes place in Fairmount Park and establishes the Philadelphia Museum of Art.

1901–1908 Philadelphia City Hall is the tallest habitable building in the world.

1912 Albert Barnes (1872–1951) meets Pablo Picasso (1881–1973) and Henri Matisse (1869–1954) in Paris, and begins to collect art.

1917 Benjamin Franklin Parkway construction begins, creating a future home for the city's most important museums.

1930 A hot-dog vendor named Pat Olivieri slaps some steak and cheese on a bun. The cheesesteak is born.

1946 A Penn professor and a lab assistant build ENIAC, the world's first computer.

1970 French chef Georges Perrier opens Le Bec-Fin, starting a Philadelphia restaurant renaissance.

1971 Kenneth Gamble (b. 1943) and Leon Huff (b. 1942) found Philadelphia International Records and establish The Sound of Philadelphia, Motown's biggest competitor.

1975 Elton John's (b. 1947) *Philadelphia Freedom* hits number one on the American pop charts.

1976 *Rocky* hits it big in the box office, then wins the Best Picture Oscar, sealing Philly's rep as hardscrabble.

1980 Phillies win the World Series of Baseball.

1985 Mayor Wilson Goode (b. 1938) authorizes the dropping of a bomb on a home belonging to MOVE, a radical black roots group, killing 11 members of the group and destroying 62 homes.

1991 Future Pennsylvania governor Edward Rendell (b. 1944) wins the mayor's race and spurs on the rebirth of Center City as a destination for dining, shopping, and bar-hopping.

1999 M. Night Shyamalan (b. 1970) releases *The Sixth Sense* and puts Philadelphia back on the film-making map.

2008 Phillies win the World Series of Baseball.

2012 The Barnes Foundation moves to the Parkway and the nearby Rodin Museum reopens, revitalizing Philly's Museum Row.

Philadelphia's **Architecture**

Like the city itself, Philadelphia's architecture and art scene is a melting pot of schools and styles. Walk down most any Center City street, and you're likely to encounter Art Deco facades, Victorian townhouses, Colonial brick buildings, freshly painted murals, and, above it all, glass-and-steel skyscrapers. Philadelphia's very first buildings were simple log cabins, which are now all but lost to time. The city's second architectural wave was more enduring: 17th-century settlers often built their houses of meeting and worship in brick, using a mix of architectural styles from their diverse backgrounds. One such brick edifice is the Old Swedes' Church (see p 23), built around 1700 and still active. The guild-built marriage of Gothic and medieval styles has nods to the then-emerging Georgian aesthetic, featuring alternating Flemish Bond brick patterns.

More examples of Georgian architecture—typified by symmetry and simplicity, paned windows and rectangular transoms—include plainly elegant Christ Church (see p 27), Carpenters' Hall (see p 26), Powel House (see p 55), and Independence Hall (see p 9).

About half a century later came the next wave of building design, a marriage of classically Greek Palladian and Georgian styles, called Federal. This style dominated important buildings from pre-Revolutionary times until the mid-1800s and can be found in four-pilastered Library Hall and the Pine Street side of Pennsylvania Hospital (see p 57), in addition to dozens of houses in Society Hill: Look for a front door surrounded by glass panes and topped by an arched window. Another sure sign of a Federal building: the presence of a bald eagle.

The next several decades subtracted the Georgian leanings from Federal architecture and revived the classically Greek. Not surprisingly, this early-19th-century architectural style is called Greek Revival—or, if you prefer, neoclassical. Architects known for this style included artist-turned-architect William Strickland (1788–1854), who designed the heavily columned, dramatically domed Second Bank of the United States; Old City's imposing Merchants' Exchange at 2nd and Walnut streets; and the National Mechanic Bank, 22 S. 3rd St. (btw. Market and Chestnut sts.), now a restaurant and bar. Similarly, architect William Haviland (1792–1852) did some of his most important work in Center City, including the Walnut Street Theater (see p 128), the University of the Arts building at broad and Pine streets, and Eastern State Penitentiary (see p 48).

Frank Furness (1839–1912), another native son, designed distinctively ornamental Victorian Gothic buildings featuring polychromatic masonry (multicolored bricked laid in an icing-type fashion), including the elegant Pennsylvania Academy of the Fine Arts (see p 30) and Fischer Fine Arts Library at the University of Pennsylvania (see p 71). Scotsman John McArthur, Jr. (1823–1890) designed the all-masonry City Hall (see p 15) in Second Empire style.

Philadelphia's earliest skyscrapers would not be considered so by modern standards. Upon its building in 1925, the Ben Franklin House on Chestnut Street, between 8th and 9th streets; 30th Street Station (see p 71); and the Franklin Institute (see p 47) were considered tall. The first modern-looking skyscraper was the steel-and-glass PSFS building (now a Loews Hotel, see p 140), designed by William Lescaze (1896–1969) and George Howe (1886–1955) in 1932, and considered the world's first International Style building. Native son Louis I. Kahn (1901–1974) served as architect for Richards Medical Library at the University of Pennsylvania, while I.M. Pei (b. 1917) designed Society Hill Towers (see p 18) and the shining National Constitution Center (see p 10). In the 1980s, chess piece–like Liberty One (1650 Market St.) and Liberty Two (1601 Chestnut St.) were the first buildings to rise above the brim of William Penn's hat atop City Hall—formerly the official cap on local building height. More skyscrapers quickly sprouted. In 2008, cable giant Comcast put its name on the city's tallest building to date, the tech-chocked, USB-stick-looking Comcast Center at 17th Street and JFK Boulevard (see p 63).

Toll-free Numbers & Websites

AIRLINES

AIR CANADA
☎ 888/247-2262 in the U.S. or Canada
www.aircanada.com

AIR FRANCE
☎ 800/375-8723 in the U.S. or Canada
☎ 0871/66-33-777 in the U.K.
www.airfrance.com

AMERICAN AIRLINES
☎ 800/433-7300 in the U.S. or Canada
☎ 0844-499-7300 in the U.K.
www.aa.com

BRITISH AIRWAYS
☎ 800/247-9297 in the U.S. or Canada
☎ 0844-493-0787 in the U.K.
www.ba.com

DELTA AIR LINES
☎ 800/221-1212 in the U.S. or Canada
☎ 871-22-11-222 in the U.K.
www.delta.com

FRONTIER AIRLINES
☎ 800/432-1359
www.frontierairlines.com

JETBLUE
☎ 800/538-2583
www.jetblue.com

LUFTHANSA
☎ 800/645-3880 in the U.S.
☎ 800/563-5954 in Canada
☎ 871-945-9747 in the U.K.
www.lufthansa.com

SOUTHWEST AIRLINES
☎ 800/435-9792
www.southwest.com

TURKISH AIRLINES
☎ 90/212-444-0-849
www.thy.com

UNITED AIRLINES
☎ 800/864-8331
www.united.com

US AIRWAYS
☎ 800/428-4322 in the U.S. or Canada
☎ 0845-600-3300 in the U.K.
www.usairways.com

CAR-RENTAL AGENCIES

ALAMO
☎ 877/222-9075
www.alamo.com

AVIS
☎ 800/633-3469 in the U.S.
☎ 800/879-2847 in Canada
☎ 8445-44-55-66 in the U.K.
www.avis.com

BUDGET
☎ 800/218-7992 in the U.S.
☎ 800/268-8900 in Canada
☎ 084-4544-3455 in the U.K.
www.budget.com

DOLLAR
☎ 800/800-4000 in the U.S. and
Canada
☎ 020-3468-7685 in the U.K.
www.dollar.com

ENTERPRISE
☎ 800/261-7331 in the U.S. and
Canada
☎ 0800-800-227 in the U.K.
www.enterprise.com

HERTZ
☎ 800/645-3131
☎ 800/654-3001 for calls from outside
North America
www.hertz.com

NATIONAL
☎ 888/501-9010
www.nationalcar.com

PAYLESS
☎ 800/729-5377
www.paylesscar.com

THRIFTY
☎ 800/367-2277
www.thrifty.com

MAJOR HOTEL CHAINS & MOTEL CHAINS

ALOFT
☎ 877/462-5638
aloft.starwoodhotels.com

BEST WESTERN
☎ 800/780-7234 in the U.S. or Canada
☎ 0800/90-44-90 in the U.K.
www.bestwestern.com

CLARION HOTELS
☎ 877/424-6423 in the U.S. or Canada
☎ 0800-44-44-44 in the U.K.
www.clarionhotel.com

COMFORT INNS
☎ 877/424-6423 in the U.S. or Canada
☎ 0800-44-44-44 in the U.K.
www.comfortinn.com

CROWNE PLAZA HOTELS
☎ 800/439-4745
www.crowneplaza.com

DAYS INN
☎ 800/225-3297 in the U.S.
www.daysinn.com

DOUBLETREE HOTELS
☎ 800/560-7753 in the U.S. or Canada
☎ 800-4445-8667 in the U.K.
www.doubletree.com

ECONO LODGES
☎ 877/424-6423 in the U.S. or Canada
☎ 0800-44-44-44 in the U.K.
www.econolodge.com

EMBASSY SUITES
☎ 800/362-2779
www.embassysuites.com

FOUR SEASONS
☎ 800/819-5053 in the U.S. or Canada
☎ 00 800/6488-6488 in the U.K.
www.fourseasons.com

HAMPTON INN
☎ 800/560-7809
www.hamptoninn.com

HILTON HOTELS
☎ 800/445-8667 in the U.S. or Canada
☎ 0800-4445-8667 in the U.K.
www.hilton.com

HOWARD JOHNSON
☎ 800/221-5801
www.hojo.com

HYATT
☎ 888/233-1234 in the U.S. or Canada
☎ 0845-888-1234 in the U.K.
www.hyatt.com

INTERCONTINENTAL HOTELS & RESORTS
☎ 800/439-4745 in the U.S. or Canada
☎ 0800/1800-1800 in the U.K.
www.ihg.com

KIMPTON HOTELS
☎ 800/546-7866
www.kimptonhotels.com

LOEWS HOTELS
☎ 800/235-6397
www.loewshotels.com

MARRIOTT
☎ 888/236-2427 in the U.S. or Canada
☎ 800-1927-1927 in the U.K.
www.marriott.com

OMNI HOTELS
☎ 888/843-6664
www.omnihotels.com

RADISSON HOTELS & RESORTS
☎ 800/967-9033 in the U.S. or Canada
☎ 0800-374-411 in the U.K.
www.radisson.com

RAMADA WORLDWIDE
☎ 800/854-9517 in the U.S. or Canada
☎ 0808-100-0783 in the U.K.
www.ramada.com

RED ROOF INNS
☎ 800/733-7663
www.redroof.com

RENAISSANCE HOTELS & RESORTS BY MARRIOTT
☎ 888/236-2427
www.renaissancehotels.com

RITZ-CARLTON
☎ 800/542-8680 in the U.S. and Canada
☎ 0800/234-000 in the U.K.
www.ritzcarlton.com

RODEWAY INN
☎ 877/424-6423
www.rodewayinn.com

SHERATON HOTELS & RESORTS
☎ 800/325-3535 in the U.S. and Canada
☎ 0800/3253-5353 in the U.K.
www.starwoodhotels.com/sheraton

SUPER 8 MOTELS
☎ 800/454-3213
www.super8.com

TRAVELODGE
☎ 800/525-4055
www.travelodge.com

WESTIN HOTELS & RESORTS
☎ 800/937-8461 in the U.S. or Canada
☎ 0800/3259-5959 in the U.K.
www.starwoodhotels.com/westin

WYNDHAM HOTELS & RESORTS
☎ 877/999-3223 in the U.S. or Canada
www.wyndham.com

Index

Photo **Credits**

Photo **Credits**

Notes